Pastor Doug thank you to bring this book

# FREE TO CHANGE

## ESCAPE FROM THE FORCES THAT KEEP YOU THE SAME

MATTHEW J. TAYLOR

This publication contains the opinions and ideas of its author. The author does not dispense medical advise or prescribe the use of any technique as a form of treatment for physical, emotional, or medical problems without the advice of a physician, either directly or indirectly. The intent of the author is only to offer information of a general nature to aid in overall well-being. In the event you use any of the information in this book for yourself or others, the author and the publisher assume no responsibility for your actions.



ISBN: 978-0-9953338-0-2 paperback
ISBN: 978-0-9953338-1-9 ebook

10 9 8 7 6 5 4 3 2 1
1st edition, October 2016

# CONTENTS

# Introduction

I wrote this book to solve three problems.

Despite being a nutritionist, I spent the better part of two years satisfying every food craving that came along. I ate muffins for breakfast, fast food for lunch, crackers for dinner and ice cream as an evening snack. In a short time, I put on nearly thirty pounds of fat and lost a lot of the muscle I had spent years earning in the gym. Although I hated the way I looked and no matter how many resolutions I made, I just couldn't seem to change.

I noticed the same thing happening in the lives of other people. In moments of either inspiration or desperation, some would beg me for help with nutrition, only to suddenly lose interest a few days or weeks later. I couldn't blame them, or really even help them, because I was doing the same thing. I felt helpless to make a difference.

Writing this book has been a way to equip myself to help others. My head was full of the practical dos and don'ts for success in life. I have attended all kinds of seminars, conferences and courses on topics like nutrition, business, relationships and faith, but they all added up to a lot of knowledge with very little action. As a result, I could give great advice, but I could rarely help with the follow through.

Finally, I wanted to understand the deeper elements of success and why some victories feel so easy while others are seemingly impossible. Why, for example, do so many successful businesspeople have so much trouble getting their weight under control? They have proven themselves to have drive, persistence and smarts, but those virtues don't seem to transfer through to the rest of their lives.

I had similar problems. When it came to achievement in school or at work, it seemed easy to stay disciplined. However, with my physical health, I just couldn't stick to a plan. Why doesn't success in one area mean you can succeed in another place? I needed to know.

We all want to make improvements to our lives in some way, whether to our health, fitness, relationships, career or other. Conveniently, we live in a world full of answers. A simple web search or trip to the bookstore can provide us with a great strategy for just about any goal. However, if it's so easy to know what to do, then why aren't we doing it? Why do we keep starting our resolutions with great intentions, but then continue to fall flat or make things worse than when we started?

In my attempts to work this out in my own life, I started by researching systems. I thought that all I needed was the right routine, and assumed nothing was working for me because I hadn't yet figured out how to build them well enough. Although I still believe in the need for great systems to facilitate change, I discovered that I needed to resolve a deeper issue: my stories.

I have come to realize that a goal is just a story that we tell ourselves about something we want. Unfortunately, it's not the only story we're telling. When that thing we desire contradicts one or more of what I consider to be the four stories of the heart, we get stuck. Creating real change requires that we escape from these hidden forces that keep us the same. We do that by getting everything inside of us to work together, all pointing in the same direction, towards the future we are meant to live.

***A goal is just a story that we tell ourselves about something we want. Unfortunately, it's not the only story we're telling.***

I'm not a psychologist or a counselor. I'm a nutritionist and marketer, fascinated by why we do what we do, and eager to make a difference in your life. I didn't go out and conduct my own research to create new theories. Instead, I have taken much of what I learned by studying neuroscience, psychology, sociology and Christian theology, and I have distilled it down to something that is practical and user-friendly.

Learning and applying the contents of this book has helped me, and others, to get free and change. If you have become frustrated with your own inability to get unstuck, then I urge you to take a step back and look at your stories. You may be surprised by what you find.

## *Take Action!*

The pages ahead are full of insights that will help you create new life stories. Put it all into practice by downloading the free worksheets at www.MyChangePlan.com.

# PART 1
# DEFINE YOUR STORIES

# CHAPTER 1
# LIFE IS STORY

It was December 24th, 1914: the first Christmas Eve of World War One. After five months of war and countless lost lives, a one-day truce began between opposing British and German troops. It started around 8:30pm when the German troops hung lanterns, called out Christmas greetings to their enemy and sang carols for all to hear. As the British soldiers heard from the other side, they cautiously joined in.

The Christmas Eve celebration eventually came to a close, but as the sun rose on Christmas Day, something even more unusual happened. German soldiers left their trenches and walked out into no man's land, shouting, "Merry Christmas" in English. As the British men looked around and saw the unarmed enemy soldiers approaching, a few left their own trenches to return the sentiment.

Soon the battleground was full of Christmas cheer. In the midst of war, enemies became friends and even exchanged gifts of cigarettes, food and souvenirs. This joy, however, did not last long. Christmas passed and the ceasefire came to an end.

So how did a spontaneous truce happen between men who were only moments before trying to kill each other? Both sides began the fight as members of their own group with different perspectives, goals and ideologies. But war was something new to them. It was a story that could be easily overruled by something more meaningful: Christmas.

The men identified with their enemy because something more unifying ran deeper than war. On that day, the British and the Germans had something in common. And as their paths crossed with the **story** of Christmas, they made a dramatic change in behaviour. In a similar way, when we discover or create a more powerful story within ourselves, we can create previously impossible change.

***When we discover or create a more powerful story within ourselves, we can create previously impossible change.***

That's ultimately what this book is about.

## The Stories In Us

Our lives are built upon stories. When you look in the mirror each morning, you tell yourself a story about how you look. As you stand before a crowd to deliver a speech, you define yourself as good or bad, and judge how well you're doing. When you approach the stranger at a networking event, you anticipate success or failure. When you come home from a long day at work and the dishes still aren't done, you make an assumption about how much your spouse really cares. We all have an ongoing conversation with ourselves.

This inner narrative is also the voice of our convictions. It is what we believe to be either true or untrue. You have a story about what it means to be healthy and whether it's possible for you to achieve it. You may have a story about politics, what party should be in office, or that all politicians are the same. You have stories about what makes a marriage, how much money you should earn and what religion you should adopt. You have a multitude of stories about who you are, what you are worth and what matters most in life.

These core heart stories, or beliefs, influence everything in our lives, regardless of the circumstances. They exist and run silently in the background of our minds, ready and waiting for action. We see everything and everyone in our lives through our own personal storytelling.

### Stories Lead & Direct

We are all in the midst of living our stories–the way that our own hearts and minds determine we should go. Everything we see, feel and hear goes through the filter of our beliefs and inner dialogue. We interpret each experience, give it a meaning and then respond in the best way that we know. It could be giving a loving embrace after receiving a gift or committing to a healthier lifestyle after seeing an overweight picture. Everything we do is directly related to the story we tell.

***Everything we do is directly related to the story we tell.***

Whether an assumption is scientifically proven doesn't matter to those who believe it. It has already become truth and is having an effect on how they think, feel and act. An extreme example is someone struggling with an eating disorder. You look at this person and see skin and bones, but the one who is struggling can only see fat. Or perhaps you think a friend is mad at you, so any good-natured teasing comes across as cold-hearted abuse. Put simply, we see what we expect to see and then act accordingly.

Let's explore the process of how beliefs become actions.

*Step 1: Belief Creates Expectation*

Every belief creates an expectation. If something is "true", then of course it's going to happen, right? If you believe your spouse loves you, then you will expect him or her to act lovingly towards you. If you believe your boss wants to fire you, then you may expect harsh or callous treatment. If you believe that your genes are making you fat, then you will expect to be overweight your entire life.

*Step 2: Expectation Directs Focus*

Once you have an expectation, your brain works to help make it happen with its Reticular Activating System (RAS). This system handles a number of functions, but its relevance here is in directing your attention and how you filter and prioritize information.[1]

Have you ever walked down a busy street filled with ads, posters and billboards, but managed to spot one small sign for discounts on travel–at the exact time you were thinking about taking a vacation–while ignoring everything else? Maybe you bought a new car that you thought was unique and suddenly began to see it everywhere you went. Or you could be at a party, deep in conversation with a good friend while ignoring the steady hum of background noise. Yet, when someone from behind says your name, your attention shifts away from the once engrossing conversation. In situations like these, your brain's RAS is presenting you with the information it thinks is most important.

Now combine this high tech filtration system with what psychologists call Confirmation Bias. We have a natural tendency to see, hear and experience things that agree with what we already believe.[2] When something doesn't line up with our expectations, we ignore and discard it.

Think about the power of first impressions. You're introduced to someone who, unknown to you, is having a bad day and is acting distracted, disinterested and a little rude. Now every time you think of this person, it's through your first impression. Although others may have a very different opinion, you have a hard time changing what you believe. Despite what others say, you keep seeing things that prove you were right in the first place.

This bias, as inconvenient as it may seem, is valuable. If your beliefs were changing on a daily basis, you would live a stressful and confusing life! To prevent that difficulty, your brain directs your focus to see and interpret life in ways that proves what you already think is true.

### *Step 3: Focus Constructs Reality*

What you see is all there is—at least to you. Dr. Andrew Newberg is a Neuroscientist at the University of Pennsylvania and a bestselling author. In an interview with NPR News, Newberg said, "The more you focus on something—whether that's math or auto racing or football or God—the more that becomes your reality, the more it becomes written into the neural connections of your brain."[3]

Your brain paints a personalized version of reality using whatever is at the centre of your focus. In other words, God becomes more real when you focus on Him, and life becomes more sweet as you practice gratitude. The world is full of unlimited possibilities. We all see and experience it differently because we each have our own individual sense of reality.

***Your brain paints a personalized version of reality using whatever is at the centre of your focus.***

*Step 4: Reality Generates Perception*

An event takes place in your life and you tell yourself a story about what it means. That narrative then becomes your interpretation of the moment. You assume the motives of the other person, what they must think of you, what his or her words mean, and so on.

Here's an example. A man comes home from a long day at work and sits down to watch TV. Just as he settles in, his wife asks him to finish the job he promised to do last week. As soon as the words leave her lips, he can feel anger and frustration building inside of him. He really isn't in the mood to do this, especially now that he's about to unwind.

The man's mind quickly spirals out of control. His blood boils as he says to himself, "Everyone always takes advantage of me! My boss keeps piling on more work. My clients call me at all hours of the day to complain and demand lower prices. And my friends always want to use my truck for help with moving. What a life!"

This negative assumption of, "everyone always takes advantage of me" isn't new to the man. He has believed this for a while and, to him, that's just the way it is. Now his wife is asking something of him, and as the experience passes through his faulty lens, he explodes at her shouting, "Why do I always have to do everything around here? It's just take, take, take!" This simple misunderstanding occurred because of a defeating perception of reality.

*Step 5: Perception Leads to Action*

What you see, whether real or not, creates a feeling. In the case above, our friend saw continued abuse from everyone in his life and reacted based on the thoughts and feelings it provoked. In short, *an event takes place, a story is told, a feeling is made and an action is taken.*

A personal story that says you are unworthy creates a sense of inadequacy, timidity and fear when meeting new people. Your response may be to leave a party early or to become irritable and standoffish. On the other hand, if you felt confident and strong going into the party, you would step into the occasion and happily meet someone new. Whichever action seems more like you is the result of the beliefs you hold and the stories you tell. Your beliefs direct how you think, feel and act.

This is an important sequence to really understand. What we believe selects what we see, which then creates our reality. We look through our personal pair of glasses and live based on how we interpret the world around us. When our core beliefs create a reality that is full of wrong assumptions, we can't help but make poor choices. We get tricked into doing things that sabotage us and leave others wondering if we're crazy. To break free from the viscious cycles and move towards a better life, we must change our hidden stories. Everything else flows out from there.

***When our reality is full of wrong assumptions, we can't help but make poor choices that sabotage us.***

## You Become Your Story

Wallace Wattles was a forerunner in understanding the power of the mind. In his 1910 book, *The Science of Getting Rich*, he wrote, "the creative power within us makes us into the image of that to which we give our attention. We are thinking substance, and thinking substance always takes the form of that which it thinks about."

Wattles was echoing Solomon's wise words, "For as he thinks within himself, so he is" (Proverbs 23:7a). In essence, we become the physical expression of a series of stories that live on the inside of us. Our attention goes where our stories lead and, as Wattles so accurately wrote, we become the physical form of our attention and thought.

If your personal story contains poverty, then you will never have great or lasting wealth. If your story includes ill health and obesity as major themes, then how can you expect to have anything else? If, on the other hand, you tell yourself a story of love, acceptance and worthiness, you begin to move in that direction instead.

Stories are so important that they even dictate the shape of your body and the quality of your physical health. Dr. Ellen Langer, a social psychologist and author of *Counterclockwise*, conducted a study in 1979 that reveals this truth. Langer took two groups of men in their 70s and 80s on a weeklong retreat that immersed them in the past. Their physical environment was full of magazines, books, news and television shows from 1959.

One group of men was instructed to act, speak and try to feel like they did twenty years earlier. They received pictures of themselves from that year and wrote autobiographies as though it was the 1950s. In contrast, the second group remained in the present time, but simply reminisced about the past. The first group lived as though it was 1959, while the second was merely remembering.

Remarkably, both groups of men encountered health improvements. However, those who fully immersed themselves in their younger years experienced the most significant results. These men enjoyed greater joint flexibility and reduced arthritis, as well as improvements in height, weight, gait and posture. They even looked noticeably younger.

One of Dr. Langer's main observations was that, "it is not primarily our physical selves that limit us but rather our mindset about our physical limits…To begin, we must ask if any of the limits we perceive as real do exist." It's clear that the dialogue between our ears is more powerful than many people realize.

The stories we tell about ourselves often place limitations on who we become and what we accomplish. The success you experience, the results you achieve and the quality of your life are all intimately connected to the stories happening below the surface.

The conclusion: Your inner stories have the power to limit your life no matter how hard you try to change. The good news, as you will discover, is that you have the ability to write something new. But before we get there, let's look at how stories are made.

## Every Story Has an Author

Your brain goes through a quick, but complex, process to form a new story. Childhood tends to set the stage for our lifelong beliefs, but it can happen at any age.

First, an event takes place and you give it a meaning. That perception, a story you tell about it, produces a feeling. When you feel good, you enjoy it and try to make it even better. When you feel some sense of pain, whether emotional or physical, you try to fix the problem and make it go away. Then, in order to prepare for the future, your brain records the whole experience and creates a pathway to better respond to similar situations when they arise.

Let's look at an example.

> **Event:** An 8 year old boy falls off his bike and skins his knee. He cries and runs to his father. The father sees his son crying and says, "It's not that bad, son. You're a big boy, stop crying."
>
> **Feeling:** The boy feels the pain of shame, believing there is something wrong with him for crying.
>
> **Response:** The boy responds by holding back his tears and hiding his emotions.
>
> **Outcome:** As a result of his response, the boy escapes the feeling of shame (PAIN) and regains his father's approval (PLEASURE).
>
> **New Story:** From this experience, the boy learns to believe that, "Real men don't show emotion," and, "crying leads to rejection."
>
> **New Pathway:** In order to prevent the pain of shame and maintain the acceptance of others, the boy's brain creates a new pathway: "If I hide my emotions, then I will be a real man and others will respect me."

As this boy grows up, he lives with the belief that he can't be emotional if he wants to be a real man. As an adult now, he feels uncomfortable and shuts down in emotional situations. He has a difficult time expressing himself to those he loves, and he never seems to feel highs or lows. All of this is because of the story he first told himself at eight years old.

## Self-Defeat is a Story

Everything we believe and do, whether positive or negative, serves a purpose. Even the stories and habits that sabotage us exist to be helpful and supportive. When an opportunity or threat arises, our stories and pathways are simply trying to get the right result as fast as possible.

Let's look at an example of how negative habits and stories try to protect us, but often, cause damage. Jimmy, a small sixth-grader still waiting for his growth spurt, gets picked as the school bully's next target. The bully confidently informs Jimmy one morning that he intends to fight him after school by the flagpole. It's a small school with only one exit and windows that are too high to climb out. If Jimmy wants to go home that day, he has no choice but to go outside and walk past the flagpole where the bully will be waiting for him.

In response, Jimmy spends the entire day in fear and goes over every possible scenario in his mind. He could tell a teacher and get escorted out, but that would only help for one day and then the bullying would just get worse. He could run right by the bully and hope to be faster than him, but again, it would only help this one time. Every option Jimmy considers seems to end the same way–with pain. All day long, all Jimmy can do is worry.

Three o-clock comes, the bell rings and Jimmy sheepishly walks outside to face the music. To both his surprise and delight, the bully doesn't show and Jimmy is utterly relieved. While logic would say that the fight didn't happen for reasons outside of his control, Jimmy's brain wouldn't be so rational.

In Jimmy's mind, the event, his response and the outcome are all connected. Although his worrying didn't actually change the bully's mind, Jimmy's subconscious thinks it did. His mind made a faulty assumption based on the limited facts he had at the time. To protect him from future bullies, Jimmy's brain creates a formula: threat from a bully + endless worrying = no fight and no pain.

As a result of this conclusion, Jimmy's automatic response to future threats becomes habitual worry. According to his brain, it worked once so it will work again. It doesn't sound logical, and as an adult Jimmy most likely knows it. The fact is many of our fears and concerns are not logical. For example, a person can know that public speaking isn't that bad, and yet feel nauseous thinking about an upcoming speech. Just because your conscious mind "knows" something doesn't mean your heart believes it.

In Jimmy's case, his adult brain continues to respond to threats in his old childhood way. Situations that seem dangerous or risky cause him to step back into his old pathway of worrying to achieve a painless result. In his heart, Jimmy has determined, "if I worry, nothing bad will happen."

This example, however, is not to say that everyone who worries does so because of a traumatic past experience. There are many reasons for why we do things, and identifying them isn't the purpose for this book. When we get stuck in old habits and confusing self-sabotage, we just need to know that a story may be working against us, trying to protect us from pain that may or may not ever happen. Then we can take the steps towards writing something new.

## When Goals Go Awry

Have you ever noticed that the past seems to have a funny way of repeating itself again, and again, and again? A string of relationships that start off on a high, but then spiral down to messy breakups. A series of new jobs that begin with promise and excitement, but quickly become too stressful and exhausting to take. Weight loss plans that help you lose 30 pounds in two months, but then you bounce back and gain 40 more.

Some call it bad luck. The truth, though, is that circumstances may change, but the hidden stories of the heart remain the same. Without correction, they will eventually draw us back to live life with the same unwanted results.

A common remedy for a "string of bad luck" or a dead-end in life is to throw everything out and start over. It might mean quitting your job, getting a divorce or selling all your possessions and moving to the other side of the world. Whatever the change, it's done in an attempt to hit the reset button on life and rebuild from scratch.

The problem is that the rebuilding process happens within the same stories–the same ways of thinking and doing. So while it may feel like a restart, it's far from it. Only your external circumstances have changed while your internal dialogue remains the same.

More often than not, the secret matters of your heart eventually produce the same results as you had before. So although that new job feels great and the grass seems green now, your ability to maintain your current positive circumstances isn't based on your intentions and desires to do so. Your success requires new circumstances along with new systems of belief. Old and negative stories will sabotage you every time.

***Your success requires new circumstances along with new systems of belief.***

When I went away to university, I saw it as an opportunity to start fresh and to make a new name for myself. I am an introvert with a love for quiet time and a built-in aversion to big crowds. Growing up, I didn't understand the difference between introverts and extroverts, so I assumed there was something wrong with me for not being like my extroverted friends. Now I know better, but at the time, I allowed my introversion to toe the line of shyness. I frequently found myself struggling to meet new people and unable to speak in large groups.

In the weeks leading up to the first day of university, I decided that things would be different this time. I would become the guy I wanted so badly to be–the center of attention and the life of the party. Unfortunately, this resolution, despite all the strength and determination behind it, lasted only until I walked into my dorm room and met my new roommates and neighbours. At that moment, old familiar feelings and insecurities returned and brought with them a recognizable sense of loneliness and frustration.

I made a lot of friends in school and many were unaware of my inner turmoil. But no matter how hard I tried, I could not get free from my insecurities or really change my life. Only when I began to address the root problems did I begin to experience lasting change. I had to uncover the destructive belief systems that were shaping my emotions, my feelings and my behaviours. I finally had breakthrough towards my true self when I learned to replace those bad stories with the empowering truth.

## Competing Stories Hold You Back

I had two competing stories within me. My logical mind wanted to become more outgoing and bold while my emotional mind was trying to keep me quiet and out of the way. My goal was pointing in one direction, but the beliefs I had about myself and my way to stay safe in a dangerous world were pointing in the opposite direction. The result of two or more opposing stories at work in your life is a standstill. In these types of situations, the best we experience is a modest success, followed by a sudden slip and fall backwards into our old ways and beliefs.

***The result of two or more opposing stories at work in your life is a standstill.***

Picture yourself sitting on a raft, drifting peacefully down a river. You decide that you no longer like the direction you're heading in, so you look back to see where you would rather go. You find a place on the distant horizon and start to paddle against the stream. As you begin, it doesn't seem very difficult, but the more you paddle, the stronger the current gets. You make a little bit of headway, but eventually tire and let the pull of the river takes you back in the same old direction.

That new destination you hoped for is much like an everyday goal. We find things in life we don't like, so we start paddling against the stream of our comfortable habits. It seems easy at first, but then our deeper stories start to compete with the goal and push against us until we fail.

In the real world this might look like going on a diet when the best way you know how to connect with those you love is by going out to eat. In this scenario, your story of trying to lose weight is fighting against your values of connection and meaningful relationships. Until these stories are able to work together, you will continually bounce back and forth between them.

Another example is the conscious desire to get a promotion at work, but a subconscious story that says you won't be able to handle the pressure if you did. These types of internal conflicts, as you can see, will do anything but allow you to advance.

If you have a list of failed goals that started with a little success but ended in disappointing failure, then you likely have competing stories working against you. This hidden conflict not only holds you back, but also makes any kind of success far more difficult than it needs to be.

## Change Your Story, Change Your Life

Because your life is the expression of your stories, it stands to reason that if you change those stories, you can change your life. This means that you have a choice to make: to become a co-author in the creation of new stories or to keep living out the same old ones that brought you to where you are now.

Life has all different kinds of both positive and negative experiences for us. We can't avoid all losses and failures, but we can author empowering beliefs that lead to more successes. If you don't like what your heart is saying, it's time to change the conversation. You can't change your past and you can't control every circumstance, but you *can* choose the stories you tell yourself.

***It's time to change the conversation.***

Changing your internal conversations is what sets you free, and it's what this book is all about. When life is interpreted and examined through faulty stories, the wrong things keep happening. However, as you begin the process of understanding, editing and leveraging the stories you have about yourself, what matters most, how the world works and your ways of living well, then your life will naturally move in a new and successful direction. Contrary to popular belief, creating the life you want isn't just about self-control. It begins with story control.

***Contrary to popular belief, creating the life you want isn't just about self-control. It begins with story control.***

**Up Next**

Now that you understand the power of beliefs, it's time to dive into the four core stories that direct our lives. First up is identity: who you say you are.

# Chapter 2
# The First Story: Identity - Who I Am

*Susan became a manager in her early twenties. She had been a model employee for several years, rising to every occasion to deliver great work. As a result, she had a reputation of being a smart young woman with a great work ethic and a bright future at the company.*

*It all began when Susan's boss called her into his office to discuss a corporate restructure. All her hard work had paid off with a promotion and her own small team. The new position and responsibility all seemed great to Susan, right up until her first day.*

*Susan was immediately uncomfortable as she walked past the team she was supposed to oversee; people who had been her peers just days ago. She entered her brand new office and her stomach sank. The previously confident young performer was suddenly feeling too small for her new shoes.*

*After a few relatively uneventful first days in her new role, Susan and her team sat down to discuss current and upcoming projects. It started off well, but soon took a turn. Susan made a controversial decision the previous day and two people on the team were in obvious disagreement. A discussion quickly broke out with strong opposing opinions. Susan, who wouldn't have shied away from a good debate before, now felt under attack.*

*She immediately shut the discussion down by blaming the decision on upper management.*

*Unfortunately, this was just the beginning of her new challenges. Susan became afraid to make difficult decisions. If she thought someone might get upset, she would defer her leadership to others. When others couldn't or wouldn't do the controversial work for her, she would hide, ignoring all phone calls and emails until her boss was brought into the loop and she had no choice but to act.*

*In addition, attending management meetings was agonizing for Susan. She felt small and insignificant in the midst of those who she believed were far smarter and more qualified to be in management. As a result, Susan remained quiet and only contributed when called upon. And even then, her contributions were short and not very insightful.*

*In a few short months, Susan had gone from all-star employee to underperforming manager and she couldn't understand why. She wanted to be a great leader and meaningful contributor, but she felt walked on by her staff, unwanted by her boss and totally incompetent in everything she did. Susan feared that if something didn't change, and soon, she would be looking for a new job.*

---

"Who am I?"

Asking this question is easy, but answering it isn't so simple. This task of uncovering our identity is difficult for two main reasons. First, it's not as effortless as writing a single statement or definition. Instead, it's a matter of seeing a full, often complicated, picture.

We have a multitude of little beliefs that combine to form our self-image. It includes a story for everything about us, like our preferences, behaviours, skills, attractiveness, intelligence and worthiness, just to name a few. In essence, there is nothing in your life unaffected by your identity.

The second challenge is that we often don't like what we see. Over the years, we learn to believe we are weak, shy, stupid, ugly, unsuccessful and unworthy of love. This may sound extreme and unlike you, but when you look in the mirror or ponder your life, are you pleased with what you see?

As a result of these two major challenges, we often try to avoid introspection and look to external factors to define us. Unfortunately, it only hurts us in the long-run. We focus on our jobs and feel small in the presence of those with bigger titles. We obsess over our possessions and feel inadequate around our wealthier friends and family. A new relationship makes us feel invincible until a disagreement makes us feel rejected. Even when we think we're on top, the sudden loss of a job, possession or relationship can send us crashing to the ground.

Achieving your goals and living with purpose begins with knowing your true identity. Because if you don't, it can all fall apart in an instant. Let's start by exploring what it is and how it influences everything you do.

## Identity is Your Property Line

You may live in a city condo with no outside yard, in a rural mansion that sits on acres of beautiful property, or perhaps somewhere in the middle. Regardless of the size of your living space and property, there is a line. Once you cross over that threshold, you step into a place that no longer feels like home, because it doesn't belong to you.

In a similar way, identity forms the boundaries of our lives, guarded by invisible fences that we learn to avoid. These limitations hide in what we believe about ourselves, manifesting as, "I can't" or I "won't" as we approach the edge of our comfort zone.

We all have an idea of what is possible for what we consider "someone like me." As we enter into a circumstance outside of that definition, we feel the stress and discomfort of stretching past our limits. As a result, we retreat back to our safety zone, where we feel comfortable and in control.

Maybe your identity is one of not exercising because you're so unfit that you believe you will only make a fool of yourself, so you say, "I can't". Or perhaps your property line prevents you from meeting new people because you know they won't like, respect or value you, so you say, "I won't".

Have you ever had a great opportunity, like a promotion or speaking engagement, but you disqualified yourself and said "no" because you felt uneasy about it? While your gut feeling can provide good instinct at times, it can also be a subconscious effort to remain safely within the limits of your property line and the confines of your small self-image.

On these occasions we miss out on amazing opportunities because we assume that we can't handle them. Regardless of how badly we want a better life, going beyond our current self-image and moving outside of our property line is stressful. Fear strikes when we expect to be exposed as "not good enough" and holds us back from God's best for our lives. It becomes a controlling force that causes us to shrink away from all that can take us to our goals. To fight this power, we must expand our boundaries.

## Identity Defines Comfort and Fit

We love it when life goes smoothly and we don't have to risk failure or feel like a fish out of water. So good, in fact, that we spend a lot of time chasing comfort and fit. We choose our circumstances, including turning down good opportunities, based on emotion. If something makes us feel ill-equipped, uncomfortable and afraid, we turn it down. Even when we are brave enough to say yes to something great, a struggling identity puts us at risk of self-sabotage.

The way you see yourself acts like a counterbalance that keeps your life in place. When you move too far in one direction or another, your identity produces resistance that brings you back into balance. You may experience an amazing success, but then your self-image rebels against the change and applies pressure to pull you back into your old ways and back to your old life.

It's easy to change your behaviour for a few days or even a few weeks. But once the initial motivation wears off, an unsupportive identity tries to force behaviours back on you that fit "people like you". Millions set weight loss goals every year. However, only a small few accomplish what they set out to do, despite the vast resources at their disposal. One reason for this problem is an identity that rejects success because being healthy or at an ideal weight doesn't fit the image.

Others spend many years looking for the perfect mate. They bounce around from relationship to relationship, trying to find "the one". Although each new romance might start off well, it ends with conflict and pain that seems to appear out of nowhere. While every case is unique, some feel so unworthy and incapable of holding a serious long-term relationship that panic strikes at the mere possibility of something meaningful. This panic then leads to a relationship sabotage that protects against the future pain of failure.

Or how about the salespeople who just can't seem to break a best month record? Finally they do, but then make irrational mistakes that blow a couple of big deals that could have taken them even further ahead.

Being at the top of your game is stressful. When that higher level doesn't fit your self-image, it doesn't feel normal, sustainable or safe. The thought of continuing upward and failing miserably is incentive enough to re-establish balance and return to what is comfortable.

## Identity Keeps You Strong and Stable

Thankfully, identity doesn't just pull you down. A healthy image has the power to hold you up. There is a skyscraper in Taiwan called the Taipei 101, which stands at almost 1,700 feet. To endure the high winds and earthquake tremors common in its area, engineers designed a 730-ton pendulum counterbalance that hangs from its ninety-second floor. This enormous sphere shifts as the building sways, helping to keep it upright and to prevent any structural damage when outside forces attempt to push or shake it over.

In a similar way, a healthy identity can be a source of emotional resilience during hard times. When you know who you really are and believe good things about yourself, you are quick to recognize life struggles as nothing more than temporary setbacks and opportunities for growth. You fight through challenges, expecting that your circumstances will eventually swing back up to the standards you have for your life.

On the other hand, those who struggle with low self-worth are more likely to identify with their poor circumstances. They see problems as the result of who they are as people, rather than as momentary challenges to overcome. They believe they deserve the pain and troubles that seem so prevalent in life, and feel doomed to live this way forever.

It's easy to fall into this trap when we're in the midst of hard times, but we must resist the urge to accept defeat. Otherwise, it drags us down and leaves us stuck in far less favourable circumstances than God wants for us.

Simply put, you cannot climb higher than who you say you are, but you also can't fall too far below it for long. You will always return to the place that best fits the mental image you have of yourself. If you want change, but remain stuck despite how much you believe, it's because your mind says you can, but your heart says you can't.

***You cannot climb higher than who you say you are, but you also can't fall too far below it for long.***

## Identity Works Through Thoughts and Feelings

Every day is full of experiences. You have them on your drive to work, in your many meetings, on the phone with friends, during high-pressure presentations or on an evening walk with your significant other. Whenever an experience such as these touches a belief, a thought and/or a feeling is produced.

I often catch myself thinking, "I can't handle this!" Most often, it has been the result of feeling overwhelmed by the volume and length of my to-do list or by the size of a new problem or opportunity. In moments like these, I reach what I believe is my personal limit and tell myself the lie that I am unable to succeed. In essence, I tell a story about myself and my ability that steals my confidence and creates feelings of stress, anxiety and worry.

Whenever we encounter a challenge, we measure its size against our self-image. If we feel bigger and stronger, we lean in and fight. When we feel smaller and weaker, we run.

***Whenever we encounter a challenge, we measure its size against our self-image.***

Your challenge might be with public speaking. If being a person with the ability to speak publically is not a part of your self-image, then you likely feel fear and anxiety when asked to address a crowd. You might even tell yourself something like, "I can't do this! I'm going to forget my words, my presentation will be boring and everyone will know that I have no idea what I'm doing." Whether or not you articulate these beliefs, they are fully able to generate debilitating fear. This is because a "successful public speaker" doesn't fit with your sense of self, and so you expect to fail.

These "Automatic Negative Thoughts", or ANTs as Dr. Daniel Amen calls them in his book, *Change Your Brain, Change Your Body*, cause a lot of problems for us. At times, it can seem as though our thoughts have taken over and are telling us who we are and what we can or cannot do, even without our consent. These are not you, but rather the manifestation of hidden beliefs that have risen to the surface in an attempt to serve and protect you. Although you can't prevent all negative thoughts, what you do with them is your choice.

ANTs are the outcome of an experience touching a belief. For example, your partner stops at a coffee shop on the way home from work and doesn't ask if you would like something. This experience, not bad in itself and likely very explainable, touches a belief in you that says, "he doesn't think about me," "he doesn't care about me" and perhaps even, "he doesn't love me." These sabotaging ANTs surface to our minds and then cause us to experience a feeling. In this case the feelings of being unloved and angry. Then, based on our thoughts and feelings, we act.

## Identity Paints Through Action

Your outer world is a reflection of your inner world. The things you say and do are often motivated by a self-image that is trying to express itself. This natural process can be a wonderful thing if you see yourself the way God does. But for many of us, this is simply not the case.

If you believe you are unworthy, unwanted or incapable, then your words and actions will prove it. If you believe that you are boring, then you will likely resist adventure. If you see yourself as inactive and lazy, then exercise will be an even greater chore. Believing you are unlovable can motivate you to end relationships before they have an opportunity to expose the real you. We all live in a way that produces the life that best reflects the inner image we hold of ourselves.

***If you believe you are unworthy, unwanted or incapable, then your words and actions will prove it.***

The good news is that as much as this truth works in our problems, it also works in our victories. If you learn to believe that you are a healthy kind of person, then it becomes much easier to make healthy choices. If you believe that you are kind, then you will find ways to be kind to those you meet. If you believe you are smart and successful, then you will act like it, too.

Whatever your goal may be, it is important that you see yourself as the one who is able and willing to do it. Otherwise, trying to force behaviours that fight against your beliefs will feel like enslavement. Your identity keeps pulling you back to the choices that produce the image. Change the picture and you change your actions.

***You must see yourself as the one who is able and willing to do it.***

## Identity Produces Assurance and Persistence

Your self-image doesn't consider how realistic or how beneficial it is to you. Whatever you believe becomes a self-fulfilling prophecy as you naturally live like it's true. Your heart will fight you every step of the way until you are convinced that the task set before you is within your ability and worthiness.

Consider the biblical story of Gideon. The nation of Israel was under fierce oppression by the Midianite nation. So much so, that their crops were regularly stolen and their livestock killed. Many were forced to live in mountain clefts and caves just to survive. Once the Israelites had finally had enough and could take no more persecution, they cried out to God for help. In response to their pleas, the angel of the LORD came down and met with Gideon under an oak tree. The first words out of His mouth were, "The LORD is with you, mighty warrior."

Now Gideon wasn't under the oak tree relaxing. He was busy

threshing wheat in a winepress for fear that the Midianites would notice and steal or destroy it. He was a man in survival mode, just trying to get by without too much trouble. In other words, he wasn't living like much of a "mighty warrior." In fact, when The Lord told Gideon that he would save the nation, his first response was, "pardon me, my lord, but how can I save Israel? My clan is the weakest in Manasseh, and I am the least in my family."

Can you relate to Gideon at this point in the story? We have all had times in our lives when we feel like we are working hard just to survive. Perhaps with fear of the future and feeling like a total failure. Like many of us, Gideon felt his anxiety levels rise as he imagined himself going way beyond his self-image and comfort zone.

God played a critical role in Israel's victory over the Midianites. But to do it through Gideon, He had to change how Gideon saw himself. Gideon couldn't have become a true hero if he continued to believe the stories of his heart, which called him the weakest and the least.

Therefore, before God could give him the mission, He had to first help Gideon see himself as a mighty warrior. The stories Gideon believed about himself had to be replaced with the truth of how God saw him. They had to expand and empower him to take on this mission.

Like Gideon, we all need to know the truth about who we are so that we can fulfill the call of God and change our lives in a significant way. When we are able to see ourselves in the right way, our willpower is able to facilitate our transformation and help us become what we want to be. In contrast, when we identify with our current habits, shortcomings and circumstances, all we are able to do is stay the same.

Taking the necessary steps to change our lives can seem either possible or impossible, depending on how we view ourselves, as well as God. As we learn to see ourselves as the ones who are able, through Christ, to accomplish our vision, we gain assurance that it can really happen. When we feel this assurance, we are willing to do the impossible. We chase after our dreams as we learn to see ourselves as the ones who can and will live the better life.

If you want to lose one hundred pounds but cannot see yourself as the "mighty warrior" who is able to resist the temptation of unhealthy foods, exercise consistently and cook healthy meals, then you will feel like a slave to a set of rules that are oppressing you. Chances are slim that you will follow through and last over the long term.

In addition to the struggle, almost every major effort to change comes with delay. We live in a fast-paced world and we want to see results in as little as three weeks, three days or even three minutes. In reality, however, there is often time between our new actions and our desired outcome. People don't gain a hundred pounds in a week, nor do their relationships break down that fast. Healing and personal growth takes time, which often causes us to quit soon after we start.

Persistence then, is our ability to endure through challenge and delay. Having persistence requires the assurance that the dream is both possible and true to self. Both of these conditions require an identity that embodies the process and the desired outcome. When you see yourself rightly, you keep fighting no matter what happens. You have the assurance and persistence required to create change that lasts.

***Persistence is our ability to endure through challenge and delay.***

## The Power of Your Memories

Now that you have an appreciation for the power of identity, let's look at how it forms. As you have learned, your subconscious mind is a storehouse of information about past experiences and their meanings. Even though you cannot consciously remember them all, they still operate in your life.

Memories come and go, and our ability to recall them is often questionable at best. Memory experts, such as psychologist Elizabeth Loftus, have found that our minds don't work like a roll of film that plays back our lives for us. Instead, it's more like a puzzle that is reconstructed each time we recall something. As a result of each reconstruction, our memories can change, moving further and further from what really happened.

However, the quality of our recollection of past events is not the focus here. Rather, we want to address the stories they created and left behind. Throughout each stage of our lives, we have many different experiences and take on a multitude of new beliefs about self, family, God and the world at large. Each one of those beliefs become a story that we then spend our entire lives trying to prove.

This idea of past events creating stories may not seem like a big deal to your logical adult mind, but consider when the majority of your beliefs were written: in childhood. The Prefrontal Cortex is the part of the brain responsible for logic and reasoning, but it doesn't fully develop until the age of twenty-five. So what are young children supposed to do with upsetting experiences? They don't have the ability to stop, take a breath and tell themselves the logical truth about what is happening. Rather, young children are in learning mode where everything they see, hear and feel is about them and immediately accepted as fact. With each experience they ask, "what does this mean about me?"

What happens then, when a young child tells himself that he is not good enough for affection? Or that he is only good enough if he works hard and does what he is told? As adults, the exact recollection of each experience may be long gone, but the interpretation lingers as a hidden memory that is at work within us. In essence, we are grownups living out the stories of our childhood.

***We are grownups living out the stories of our childhood.***

## Factors of Authorship

We all have defining moments that shape the way we see ourselves. Maybe you felt ignored by a parent, unwanted by friends, or unattractive compared to others. Perhaps you discovered that hard work could earn affection or that your natural athleticism won respect and friendships. All of these experiences plant little seeds of belief that produce fruit all throughout your life.

Your past is full of references about yourself. It provides evidence from what you have thought, said, done, accomplished and failed in. Everything from a broken relationship in your youth to a successful sales call as an adult is part of your identity story. Some things are ignored and others are amplified, all in an attempt to paint a self-portrait. You make some assumptions, you gather your proof and then you live as though it is all true.

Your life is a journey of self-discovery. While on that journey, you look for clues that explain why life happens the way it does and what it must mean about you. The messages that manage to get through to your heart are often the result of one or more of three factors: authority, emotion and repetition.

*The AUTHORITY Factor*

Have you ever had someone tell you something that you refused to believe? It was so clear to you that this person was wrong. But only until an "expert" said the exact same thing and you suddenly believed it. For example, a nutritionist said those foods were not as healthy as you thought, or a mentor offered advice for a healthier marriage.

This is the result of authority. When someone without it (at least in your eyes) gives advice, you pay no attention. However, when you perceive that person as having authority, it becomes so easy to accept. The more authority you attribute to someone's opinion, the more power it has to change your mind about anything, including about yourself.

This can be a teacher who says you will never pass the class, or a doctor who labels you as sick and depressed. Perhaps a parent told you that you would never amount to anything, or a person you admired ignored you unless you did what you were told. All of these are examples of how the people we trust and respect can change the way we see ourselves.

On the opposite side, these people can also influence us for the better. The teacher can encourage his students and draw out the hidden genius in each of them. The doctor could explain that her patient is not doomed to lifelong illness, and that we all have the power to shape how our lives unfold. The parent can identify the strengths of the child and build him or her up rather than holding on to a generic standard. We can learn to believe in ourselves when someone in authority believes in us first.

We expect from ourselves what others expect, especially with those in authority. We all have different strengths and weaknesses, and simple encouragement from an authority figure won't magically change our circumstances. However, many of us live well below our true genius because no one told us that it's possible to do and be more. When those we admire elevate our own opinion of ourselves, we become greater in everything that we do. In contrast, when they deflate or neglect us, we settle for far less than our true potential.

***Many of us live well below our true genius because no one told us that it's possible to do and be more.***

*The EMOTION Factor*

In addition to the authority given to a person, the emotional intensity of an experience can leave a lasting mark. Any time you mix words or actions with enough emotion, you have the recipe for a new belief.

Think of an emotional low in your life when you were unsure of what to think or believe. At these times, we are much more likely to allow others to influence than we would normally permit. When we feel fear, uncertainty or large amounts of stress, we look for help to explain the situation.

When a confident person is called a failure for losing a job, the lie can feel true. In that moment, the self-esteem armour is down and those words offer an explanation for what happened. If a young girl gets dumped and is soon after called ugly, there is a higher than normal chance that she will believe it. If a boy fails math and his little sister teases him about being stupid, he may start to accept it as fact.

In these highly emotional times, we seek meaning and reason for what happened. We open up and accept new things about who we are that would otherwise never cross our minds. We define ourselves not simply because of an experience, but by how it makes us feel and the way we choose to interpret it. Often, those interpretations come with a little "help" from other people.

*The REPETITION Factor*

Authority and emotion are the most powerful of the three factors, but they matter less and less in the presence of repetition. If you hear "you're stupid", "you're weak" or "you're worthless" again and again, it will likely sink in and begin to shape how you view yourself. It's only a matter of time.

As you can see, your identity story is written with a lot of help from others. The big problem is that many of them don't know what they're doing. Without realizing it, they help to create and support the negative messages that defeat us. And as those unhealthy stories build up, they conceal our true identities.

***As unhealthy stories build up, they conceal our true identities.***

## Your Identity Package

Your self-image is a multitude of beliefs. But despite their vast number, you can distill them down to two statements and three questions.

*Statement #1: I am...*

The "I am" statements are your overarching assumptions about who you are. We use these statements to define ourselves as we relate to the outside world.

Some examples include: I am…

- strong
- weak
- beautiful
- ugly
- accepted
- alone
- healthy
- fat
- prosperous
- poor
- a success
- a failure
- active
- lazy
- brilliant
- stupid
- fun
- boring

*Statement #2: I'm the kind of person who...*

The "I'm the kind of person who" statement describes behaviours that you believe reflect your nature. They are the many ways you express your unique self. When you identify with something and see it as a part of who you are, you cannot help but act it out. When these statements are healthy, they cause self-expression. However, when they are unhealthy, they can act as restrictive and destructive labels.

Some examples include: I'm the kind of person who…

- lies under pressure
- enjoys exercise
- always arrives on time
- always tells the truth
- never follows through
- overreacts in conflict

*Question #1: Is this me?*

Part of the art of fulfillment in life is finding and doing the things that feel like a "fit" for you. Whenever a new opportunity comes along, one of the first things we ask ourselves is, "Is this me?" In other words, can we see ourselves doing or being it?

"This just isn't me" is a common frustration that stems from violating our sense of self. Whenever you want to make a change in your life, this question will work to either support or obstruct your efforts. If you are unable to see yourself embodying the end result, or even as the one doing the work to get there, your heart will stand firmly in your way.

***If you are unable to see yourself embodying the end result, your heart will stand firmly in your way.***

*Question #2: Am I enough?*

After you determine that a new action or opportunity really is a good fit for you, dive down into an even deeper question with, "Am I enough?" This is especially true when it comes to pressing beyond your comfort zone as the stress forces you to second-guess the decision. The pressure of moving beyond your self-image is enough to make you question your ability and worth.

***The pressure of moving beyond your self-image can make you question your ability and worth.***

Changing your life will always present problems of some kind. The determining factor of whether or not you push through the fear and enter the promise is your ability to see yourself as smart enough, beautiful enough, resourceful enough, committed enough and so on. Of course we must depend on God to help fill in the gaps of our weaknessess, but if the answer to this question is always "No", then you will be hard-pressed to go the distance.

*Question #3: Am I safe?*

Regardless of how much a new lifestyle fits your sense of self and your perceived ability, you ultimately need to feel safe for change to last. We often find creative ways to mask our hurts and protect ourselves from more of the same pain. Some people gain weight to avoid feeling objectified or to prevent abuse from others. Some sabotage their relationships before rejection and hurt can happen. And some waste their money to avoid the pressure of managing wealth.

We all want change until we think it might hurt too much. If your current lifestyle is protecting you from a perceived threat, then change removes that sense of protection and opens you up to danger. When that happens, you lose our emotional endurance to finish the race.

***We all want change until we think it might hurt too much.***

**Up Next**

Your identity is the most fundamental story of the four. Everything else is layered on top to express this inner image. Next up is values. When you understand what drives you most, you can leverage it to motivate and support change.

# Chapter 3
# The Second Story: Values - What Matters Most

*David was a new father. He and his wife Amanda had waited a few years after getting married before deciding to have kids, but when the time finally came, they both felt ready and excited for parenthood. Soon after his child was born, David started to struggle with the changes that he felt had suddenly been thrust upon him.*

*Before having their daughter, David and Amanda led very active lives. Every free moment they had meant spending time outdoors. Weekends were filled with running, biking, camping and the like. Both David and Amanda were aware that having a child would mean putting some of their extracurricular fun on hold, and the excitement of becoming a dad made David think it would be easy to give up.*

*Six months after the birth of Samantha, David's excitement was starting to wear off. Every day was the same; wake up, go to work, come home, help with the baby, go to bed, repeat. Of course he loved his daughter more than anything, but if David was being honest with himself, he felt like something was missing.*

*David didn't feel right about spending free time with friends when Amanda was busy at home with the baby. However, it was easy for him to justify spending longer hours at the office. For David, work gradually became the new outlet for the sense of adventure and conquest that he had once received from the activities he gave up. He eagerly took on more and bigger projects that sometimes required travel and often caused him to lose track of time. As unlikely and uncharacteristic as it was, David was becoming a workaholic.*

*The more David worked, the more frustrated Amanda felt. She was at home alone with the baby all day, and increasingly, well into the evenings as well. David's travel schedule was also picking up and this meant that her husband was away for as long as a week at a time.*

*David's new found love for his work wouldn't have been such a huge problem for Amanda if she had been able to expect it. The main issue was that before the baby, David never worked so much. And now, when she needed him most, he was never there. This left Amanda feeling like David was unhappy with his new life as a father and that he was avoiding his family.*

*The opposite, however, was true. David loved being a husband and father and he wanted to be great at both. But at the same time, he felt that this often meant he had to give up everything else he had previously enjoyed. David valued adventure and excitement and he needed to find a way to meet these needs that didn't result in neglecting his family.*

---

You were made to care and to live from your values. Your own personal value system is what leads you and motivates many of your decisions. It determines what you believe is right or wrong, governs every thought that you have, weighs every action you take and prioritizes every role and relationship in your life.

Your values are always at work, either for or against you. They energize and satisfy you when supported, but ignoring them can take an emotional toll. Until you gain insight into your own personal and unique value system (the things that you determine are most important in life), your attempts at change can leave you feeling depleted, unfulfilled and at odds with yourself.

Let's start by looking at what values can do for you and your efforts to change.

### Values Start with Why

A goal is just a promise with a price tag. In order to pay the price to achieve your goals, you need the currency called, "why." Many people begin each year with great intentions and a resolution to change their lives in some way. However, few are able to follow through because they fail to attach a reason that is meaningful enough to carry them to the end.

***To pay the price to achieve your goals, you need the currency called, "why".***

A goal without the why will almost never succeed. It stays on the surface as an "I want to", while a goal that runs deeper is an "I must". The main problem with a want is its weakness in the face of an impulse. One minute you want to be healthy and then the next you want to feel better with food. Or perhaps one minute you want a strong relationship, while the next you want to be right.

When we lack a compelling reason, the pressure of temptation or the pull of an old habit becomes too great to pass up. In those moments, we no longer want to pay the price for our goals. To succeed, you must ask yourself why your goal matters so it turns from a "want" into a "must". For example, a weight loss goal that says, "I want to lose weight" is much less powerful than, "I must lose weight to see and enjoy life with my grandchildren."

Everything of significance comes with a price tag. Whether it's your time and energy to exercise and prepare better foods, your raw determination to save more money each month or your self-imposed humility to apologize for the sake of your relationship, it all comes at a cost. You either have to endure pain or give something up that would provide you pleasure in the moment.

Those who have a powerful "why" have reason to fight. They are willing to make those sacrifices, even if it will cause momentary discomfort. These people identify their highest values and connect them to their goals. As a result, they experience the emotional empowerment required to make the right choices in difficult moments.

A new weight loss program, for example, promises that you will lose 30 pounds and finally be happy. While the promise is nice, the program is full of new choices and actions that change your schedule. As you experiment with each new behaviour, you have to decide if it's worth the aggravation. Exchanging old habits for new ones is uncomfortable, and if it doesn't connect with you on an emotional level then it will rarely stick.

In the end, a goal on its own is just an achievement with a set of perceived promises. It is an outcome that would be nice to have, as long as it doesn't require too much from you. But when a goal serves the purpose of expressing your core values, then it becomes something more. It becomes a must. You suddenly have the emotional lasting power to fight. From this place, you are able to endure the pain, delay the gratification and do what it takes to reach the finish line.

## Values Kill the Killers

Every significant change comes with obstacles. External ones include temptations from your environment, the financial cost of healthier habits or close friends and family who don't support the change.

These outer forces can be easy to identify, but the internal ones are not. They are silent killers that pop up suddenly to carry you away from your goals before you even realize something is happening. Thankfully, you can put a stop to them by living according to your values and doing what matters most.

Consider these four goal killers before they launch their next attack.

### *Killer #1: Total Exhaustion*

Most of us have experienced some level of burnout or exhaustion in our lives. In this state everything is frustrating, your mood is always down and all you want to do is abandon your commitments and start life over again. Even the things you once loved to do become a chore, and the smallest challenges feel impossible to overcome.

When you're in this headspace, survival becomes more important that growth because it feels like you're just getting by. Sure it would be nice to volunteer for projects that would help to advance your career or to follow through on the healthy meal plan that you created. But with no emotional fortitude left, there is no way these things will happen.

Even the world's greatest plan is meaningless if you don't have the energy to make it happen. Survival mode puts you in a short-sighted mindset, where you couldn't care less about the five-year impact of a single choice. All you really want to do is ease the pain you feel right now. You become far more interested in doing what hurts the least, rather than what matters most.

What do values have to do with it? Research shows that being true to yourself and living in alignment with your deepest values can help reduce the burnout caused by what specialists have termed, "intense emotional work."[1] Amazingly, doing what matters on an emotional level helps to protect you from exhaustion. Rather than stealing your energy, it adds to it, giving you the ability to make the hard choices when you would otherwise be too tired and too burnt out to do so.

***Doing what matters on an emotional level helps to protect you from exhaustion.***

*Killer #2: Weakened Willpower*

Contrary to popular belief, willpower isn't always available to us. Your ability to control your behavior and to carry out your decisions, like a muscle, can get tired and give up. Your willpower gets a workout every time you make a choice, fight a habit, control an urge, push yourself physically, and with all other forms of self-control.[2] With each challenge you overcome, the less strength you have left to exert over the next one. This process of willpower fatigue is called Ego Depletion.

You may have experienced Ego Depletion when you got home from work after an exhausting day. Despite your weight loss goals, you couldn't help but have two large servings of pasta for dinner, followed by a big bowl of ice cream. Among other reasons, you exhausted your willpower that day. You made hundreds of small decisions in the form of answering emails or staff and customer questions. You also practiced self-control by resisting the fatty burger at lunch and going for a salad instead. Each choice that you make, some more than others, take from your self-control, making later decisions even more difficult. Add in mental fatigue from a long, stressful day and you have the perfect recipe for making poor choices.

When your willpower tank is running on empty, you just want to do whatever feels the best, because resistance requires more energy than you have left to give. In those tough moments you lose perspective and fail to do what would move you forward in the direction of your goals.

***When your willpower tank is running on empty, you just want to do whatever feels the best.***

Thankfully, living your values can also counteract Ego Depletion.[3] Similar to emotional burnout, the hard choices energize you when they serve a purpose deeper than the inconvenience of the moment.

*Killer #3: Misguided Rewards*

As you accomplish more and move towards your goals, the urge gets stronger to cheat "just a little bit". There is nothing wrong with preplanned rewards and breaks to maintain your resolve, but anything more is Moral Licensing. The thought in your mind might be, "I've been saving really well, so I think I'll go buy a new outfit" or, "I had salad for lunch so I'll have fast food for dinner." This feels like you are getting ahead, but you are really making no progress at all.

Interestingly, Moral Licensing doesn't stop with these types of decisions. Even the option of a healthy choice makes you more likely to make a bad one. Psychologist Kelly McGonigal explains in her book *The Willpower Instinct*, that Moral Licensing is why the addition of salads to the McDonald's menu increased the sale of Big Macs. When your brain senses the presence of an opportunity to do right, it gets the same signal as if you actually did it! As a result, you feel virtuous, even though you didn't do anything. You not only want to reward yourself for doing such a "good job", but you're also more likely to trust your impulses because you "know what you're doing."

***When your brain senses the presence of an opportunity to do right, it gets the same signal as if you actually did it!***

Moral Licensing is also at work across different areas of your life. For example, you can help an elderly woman cross the street and then go treat yourself to a donut. The two were completely unrelated, but because you feel so good about yourself for what you did, it seems ok to seek out a reward.

Go ahead and reward yourself for a job well done. But make an effort to stay conscious of what is causing your good feelings and what your happy brain chemicals are tempting you to do. As you maintain a focus on what truly matters to you, and why you have set your goal in the first place, a momentary good feeling will not have the same power to send you into poor choices.

*Killer #4: Sudden Stops*

Have you ever been making progress towards a goal, but then gave into temptation in a weak moment and decided to stop and start again tomorrow or next week? Maybe you had an unhealthy breakfast so you allowed yourself fast food for lunch because the day was already ruined. You assumed that you had failed, so you might as well just quit trying for the rest of the day.

This is a very real problem for a lot of people. It can seem like making a single mistake has blown all potential progress for the day, but it's not true. Allowing small setbacks to defeat you only takes you further and further away from the end result. The truth is, every little bit matters.

Immediately after a slip up, values can come to the rescue. Just because you made a mistake doesn't mean you have to start over at a later date. Instead, acknowledge what you did, determine what you will do differently next time and then move on. When you keep your core values in mind, it becomes easier to clear your head, refocus and keep moving towards your goal.

## Values Produce Tension

In his book, *The Path of Least Resistance*, Robert Fritz writes about how our lives move in different directions because of invisible tension. He explains that even the simple act of saying "hello" puts tension on the other person to close the gap by responding with "hello" in return. As Fritz illustrates, like a rubber band, the more tension that is placed upon us, the more likely we are to act to reestablish the balance we crave.

When it comes to values, the tension is that of injustice. You have been made with a conscience that wants justice. Whether you are involved in feeding the homeless, rescuing victims of the sex trade industry or joining in the fight against cancer, there is something in each of us that gets upset when life seems unfair. We feel compelled to fight for different causes because we have different values, but we are all driven by the same inner tension of injustice.

The gap between your standard and your current state is what creates this value-based tension. When you have a strong conviction for what is right, you have a natural tendency to fight for it. It awakens a sense of passion and determination that can push you through any circumstance or challenge that stands in your way.

As a result, when you have a clear standard, nothing else will do. You become emotionally invested in living it out because it becomes a part of you. We are all experts at justifying poor choices, but when you choose to raise your standards and value something greater, you activate your conscience to play a supporting role. You no longer live in the grey zone where things are up for interpretation and you can find ways to make poor choices make sense. Instead, you see things in a way that is more black and white, where your values are either met or they are not.

The most successful weight loss programs have less to do with the meal plan and more to do with the deeper reasons why. For many, it has to do with getting healthy for their kids or grandkids. A father may want to walk his daughter down the aisle and a mother may realize that she is unable to care for her kids the way she wants to while in her current state. Both are able to feel the stress of not having what they value and are compelled to do something about it.

The injustice you feel when compromising what you value most is a powerful motivator to produce lasting change. When you connect deeply with what is already in your heart, you enlist your emotions to join forces with your head and pull you in the right direction.

## Value Types

Now that you have an appreciation for the importance of values, it's time to get practical. Your personal value system touches absolutely everything in your life and is completely unique to you. Much like your identity, it has many different parts that form a complete picture.

The following list of C.O.R.E. values are not intended to overload you, but rather to give you some insight into what is at work in your life.

### *Value Type C - Categories*

Our lives are composed of basic categories, like pieces of a pie that combine to form our entire existence. Some lists are as big as fifteen or more, but I prefer to keep it simple at only seven. They are Relationships, Health, Recreation, Spirituality, Wealth, Career/Work and Social/Community.

The amount of attention you give to any one area is largely dependent on the season of your life. A young person may focus more on relationships and career as he tries to build a family and provide for them. Someone in retirement, however, may give herself to social contribution and recreation. No longer working, she shifts her values toward something else. Although different seasons and circumstances may cause a person to focus more intently on certain categories over others, it is important to remember that your spirituality can and should spread into every other area of your life throughout every season.

These categories of our lives draw our energy and attention. We become invested in certain ones, desiring to see them grow and improve. When we find a way to attach our current goals to the area of our lives that we want to see flourish, we become more energized to overcome whatever challenges stand in the way.

*Value Type O - Others*

Other people can be the most powerful motivators in our lives. Even if we don't care enough to do something for our own benefit, we find it easier to do it for the sake of someone we love. These are the people that you care deeply about and want to support. It may be a child, grandchild, sibling, parent, spouse or best friend. If they stand to gain from your success and/or lose from your failure, then you are far more likely to stick with your plan.

*Value Type R - Roles*

We all fill many roles in life. It starts with being a son or daughter, and perhaps a brother or sister. As you get a little older, you become a friend. And then, for many, you become a father or mother yourself. Other roles include things like provider, protector, business owner, nurturer, artist, athlete, manager or employee.

As a whole, all of your roles combine to become your platform to the world. You may have some roles out of obligation, but there are likely others that you love. These positive roles are the ones that excite you and make you feel alive. If something is going to sabotage your ability to fulfill the needs of a valued role, you become more resolved to fight the battle and pay the price to protect what you love.

*Value Type E - Expression*

Expression is an overarching term. It governs how you operate throughout your daily life in everything you do. It defines what is most important in the unique expression of who you are, and it becomes the scale by which you judge every experience. It decides what is appropriate, safe, right, wrong, urgent or unnecessary. This is where you make many of your day-to-day decisions.

These governing values include character traits, needs and things. They form what you are subconsciously driven to produce. They shape how you respond to conflict, how hard you work for a promotion and what you eat after a setback.

Here are some examples of different Expression values.

> **Character Traits:** honesty, loyalty, bravery, persistence, compassion, fairness, self-control, integrity, respect, gratefulness.
>
> **Needs:** achievement, adventure, challenge, excitement, learning, stillness, stability, love, human connection, making a difference, pleasure, significance, novelty, creative expression, personal growth, financial freedom.
>
> **Things:** money, possessions, facts, evidence, faith, truth, influence, forgiveness.

You may classify things differently in your own mind, and that's fine. I find that lists help to give a more holistic picture of your value system. The important thing to realize is that they all intermingle and work with or against each other. In essence, they are all prioritized.

## Values are Prioritized

Your lifestyle is a collection of priorities. As you know, you have an infinite number of ways you can spend your time. However, there are not enough hours in the day or even days in your life to do all that you want, so you are forced to create priorities. You decide what is most important and then you do it.

In a similar way, we prioritize our values. Every decision is a matter of choosing one value over another. That choice can be as black and white as achievement verses rest or as subtle as human connection verses health. The two or more values battle it out in the heat of a moment, sometimes creating a lot of stress and anxiety. But in the end, the value with the highest priority wins most of the time.

You are a living, breathing set of beliefs and values. Every one of your behaviours serves the purpose of acting out a belief or satisfying a value. Every time you say no to a delicious, but unhealthy, treat, you value your health more than the immediate gratification. When you decide not to buy the amazing new suit or dress, you are living out your value of future financial freedom over fashion and outward image. When you tell a lie to close a business deal, you are saying no to honesty and yes to wealth or achievement.

I have been one of the worst offenders of competing values. As a nutritionist, I am very aware of what makes up a healthy diet. I know the right foods, when to eat them and how to prepare them to best preserve their nutritional content. I also believe wholeheartedly in the necessity of an active lifestyle. However, just like all the overweight doctors and divorced marriage counselors, knowledge simply isn't enough.

For two years of my life, I completely neglected my health. I quit exercising and I started eating whatever I wanted, whenever

I wanted. I certainly didn't want to gain thirty pounds, but it happened. A big part of me still valued health, but I got lost in a series of poorly prioritized values.

The majority of my poor food choices involved unhealthy lunches and snacks at work, followed by eating out for dinner with friends. I was struggling for a variety of reasons. First, I was feeling busy and often rushed each day, so I chose the convenience of buying lunch instead of taking the time to make it. Next, I realized that lunchtime was my main opportunity to get out of the office with a friend. It was my time to get human connection as well as a mental break from my work. In the same way, my unwholesome dinners were also satisfying the values of convenience and human connection instead of health.

We will compromise a low ranking value if we believe it is necessary to satisfy a higher one. You may value your family, but if your career provides a much needed sense of significance, then your relationships may take a back seat. If you are always late to meetings, then you may be valuing accomplishment over honour. Every action serves a purpose, so with every decision you make, it's important to ask yourself, "What am I saying YES to?" as well as, "What am I saying NO to?" These two questions will help to give you a clear picture of what is really at work.

***We will always violate a low ranking value if we believe it is necessary to satisfy a higher one.***

### Starving Values Find a Way

In our attempts to keep up with the fast pace of everyday life and to fit into the model of success that we set for ourselves, we often neglect our values. A young man can grow up with a love for the outdoors, but now that he has a "real job" and a young family, he settles into a simple daily routine with no adventure. A woman can value emotional intimacy yet in her desire for companionship, enters into a relationship that lacks the connection and acknowledgement that she desires. In both cases, important needs are not met. When this happens for too long, the needs often rise to the top of the priority list and lash out in unhealthy ways.

Consider your body, which needs regular nourishment to function properly. When you attempt a starvation diet and eventually give in to uncontrollable cravings, it's not because you have weak willpower. Rather, it is because every cell in your body is starving for energy and every impulse on the inside of you is trying to satisfy that need. All anyone can do at this point is give in and eat the first thing in sight.

The same holds true for your deepest values. When you neglect one for too long, it acts out and satisfies itself with a candy bar equivalent. Much like a child, when a value doesn't get the attention it needs, it lashes out. As far as it's concerned, even bad attention is better than no attention at all.

Consider these examples of starving values.

| The Value | The Shortcut |
|---|---|
| Significance | Controlling, aggressive and refuse to be wrong so people will know that you're "important". |
| Acceptance | People pleasing so others won't reject you for being different. |
| Stability | Overeating, binge drinking or extreme control over self (e.g. anorexia) in order to exert some level of control in the midst of what feels like chaos. |

| The Value | The Shortcut |
|---|---|
| Financial Security | Greed and hording to prevent loss, rather than produce wealth. |
| Adventure | Serial dating and excessive shopping or partying in an attempt to seek novelty and thrill, because everything else in life feels dull. |

You have been designed with a unique set of values and needs that must be supported. If you live a life that doesn't satisfy them in healthy ways, you will naturally find unhealthy shortcuts to fill the holes.

***If you live a life that doesn't satisfy your values in healthy ways, you will naturally find unhealthy shortcuts to fill the holes.***

**Up Next**

Your identity and values form a clear picture of how things are working on the inside of you. Next we'll explore how your perception of the outer world is playing a critical role in your victories and failures as well.

# Chapter 4
# The Third Story: Worldview - How It All Works

*Jim knew he needed to improve his health. Over the past few months he started waking up totally exhausted and a little out of breath. He had developed a persistent cough that just wouldn't go away and he would get unusually winded with simple activities like going up a few stairs.*

*At first Jim assumed he had caught a bug from his 4-year-old grandson William. William was in daycare and often brought things home that quickly passed through the family. After three months of no improvement, Jim went to his doctor for a prescription. To Jim's surprise, it wasn't so simple.*

*Over the course of 50 years Jim had paid little attention to good nutrition. He never cared to exercise and often finished off his day with a few drinks. Now Jim was suffering from clear signs of heart disease and his doctor urged him to make a number of serious changes. He needed to lose 30 pounds, cut out his high sugar intake, eat more fruits and vegetables, and stop drinking entirely.*

*Jim's wife, Patty, was horrified when he brought the news home. She quickly jumped on board with the doctor's directive and started researching food and exercise plans for both of them. At first, Jim was somewhat willing to participate in what he perceived as torture, but it didn't take long for him to start sneaking snacks and drinks when Patty wasn't looking.*

*After three months of no weight loss or health improvements, Patty got suspicious. When she discovered his secret stash, she was furious. "How could he possibly not want to change?" she thought. "Doesn't he care enough to live? If not for himself, then for me and the family."*

*When Patty confronted Jim, the truth came out. Jim didn't want to die young, but to him, the damage was already done and there was no use trying to correct it. Decades of an unhealthy lifestyle and the fact that his father had died from a heart attack at a fairly young age led Jim to believe that his fate was already sealed. In Jim's mind, there was nothing he could do about the situation, so he might as well enjoy what little time he had left. Besides, men don't eat green things; they eat meat. Salad, to Jim, was for women and rabbits.*

---

We all have our own unique way of seeing the world and understanding how it works. Your personal perspective of all that goes on around you is called a paradigm. This word, taken from the Greek word *paradeigma*, means a pattern, model or representation. It is a mental map or blueprint for navigating through life.

Our worldviews act as filters that influence everything we see and do. Without realizing it, we live as though our own mental model is the only version of reality that exists, which can get us into serious trouble at times. But when we learn to observe and change our worldview stories, the effect can be dramatic.

## Different Worldviews Create Different Experiences

Consider two men who experience identical accidents. Badly injured, both go through intense physical therapy but never fully recover. They now have to live each day with chronic pain. While both men endured the exact same event, they had two very different experiences.

The first is grateful to survive and receive a second chance at life. He reevaluates everything and decides to eliminate the nonessentials so he can focus his life on what really matters. He quits the job he doesn't like, starts mentoring at-risk kids and begins a healthy exercise and eating plan. His pain becomes a daily reminder of how much God loves him and how fortunate he is to be alive.

The second man, however, becomes angry and bitter about his bad luck in life. In the weeks and months that follow his accident, he becomes more and more depressed, turning to food and alcohol to cope. His job and relationships begin to suffer as everyone around him is either ignored or verbally abused. For him, the pain becomes a daily reminder of how much he feels God hates him.

Both men are seeing what their Confirmation Biases allow. If you remember from the first chapter, when we have a belief, our brains find plenty of evidence to prove it, regardless of how illogical it may seem. These accident survivors had different beliefs about themselves, God and the world around them. The man who believed that God is good and life is full of opportunity responded with gratitude and chose to invest in what matters most. The other man responded with anger and bitterness, because he saw his life through a very different lens.

***When we have a belief, we find plenty of evidence to prove it, regardless of how illogical it may seem.***

It's amazing how differently we interpret our experiences when we have different worldviews. The way we view life then shapes what we do. We make a conclusion based on what we expect to see and then we act, thinking that our actions are not only justified, but also necessary.

In short, we act as if what we see is all there is to see. Someone who believes that politics is full of corruption will find evidence of foul play, and may choose not to vote. Those who think that school is only for people with high IQ's might decide to drop out because they'll never make it. A person who believes that others are inherently good is quick to forgive and move on. We believe, then see and then act.

***We act as if what we see is all there is to see.***

Let's dive right in to two worldview types.

## Worldview Type 1: THE WAY IT IS

*The Way It Is* worldview is our idea of how the world works at all times. We have our own unique way of seeing the world, but we often fail to recognize that it really is just our own. Instead, we believe that our perspective is as certain as natural laws like gravity. Regardless of the truth of our assumptions, we tie ourselves up to them and live within their boundaries, which are often more like prison walls.

***We live within the boundaries of our worldview, which are often more like prison walls.***

These beliefs, in our own minds, are non-negotiable. They are what they are and there is no need to act against them or try to change them, because we think it would only be futile. With equal certainty of knowing gravity will pull us down, we surrender to invisible and often false beliefs that restrict our potential.

If you believe that people will always hurt you, you are more likely to keep all of your relationships at arm's length than you are to challenge the belief and let someone in. If you think genetics determine your fate, then you will be tempted to ignore the influence you do have on your own health. As we accept more and more false beliefs about how the world works, we must work harder and harder to survive. We force ourselves to cope with challenges that only exist in our minds.

***We force ourselves to cope with challenges that only exist in our minds.***

When we have a disempowering worldview, we feel stuck and do very little to change our situation. We think, "Why bother when the obstacle is immovable?" As a result, we give up our right and responsibility to create change and we settle for less than God's best. Too many people, as a consequence of debilitating worldviews, lose their hope and reason to fight.

While there are countless examples, let's address what I believe to be three key mindsets. Shifting your perspective on just one of them can have a big impact on your life.

### Mindset #1: Growth vs. Fixed

Carol Dweck is a professor of psychology at Stanford University. After years of research into the areas of achievement and success, Dweck condensed her findings into a book called *Mindset*. Throughout the text, Dweck introduces and explains the difference between two primary and opposing mindsets: Fixed and Growth, that have the power to control our effort and our results in life.

As Dweck explains, people with a fixed mindset believe that we are all born with a predetermined amount of ability and intelligence. They assume that if they cannot do something well now, then they never will. As a result of this flawed thinking, they are likely to reject opportunities to learn and grow because anything difficult has the very real potential to prove their inadequacy.

A fixed mindset is a big killer in many attempts to create change. When we believe deep down that anything hard will end in failure, we don't have much choice but to give up when the going gets tough. Combine the learning curve of doing something new with old conflicting habits and you're set for a challenging road ahead. So why put in all the effort when it will all be for nothing in the end?

A fixed mindset is often hidden from our conscious awareness. It works behind the scenes to make us feel uncomfortable with change and incapable of following through to victory. It is a hidden story that causes us to give up, even when we truly want a better life.

Maybe you did poorly on a test and judged yourself to be stupid. You may have had an essay or business report checked over by someone else and it was returned full of red ink and suggestions. Did you take the suggestions as an opportunity to improve your work or did it crush you and make you want to quit?

When we blame our personality for our mistakes and assume that this is simply our lot in life, we are giving in to what Dweck calls fixed thinking. When we attempt to lose weight with little or no success, and project that failure onto future programs, we are settling into a fixed mindset. Whatever your current challenge in life, if it feels permanent because of an inborn deficiency, then you need to shift your thinking.

***If a problem feels permanent because you were born this way, then you need to shift your thinking.***

In contrast to the fixed mindset, those with a growth mindset believe in self-improvement because to them it's actually possible. They understand that effort and learning can make them smarter and better at what they do. They welcome opportunities to learn and grow, because they know that where they are now is not the limit of their potential. It is merely a place along the road to something greater.

To the growth-minded person, life is not a set of achievements. Rather, it is an ongoing process of learning. These people approach change fully aware of the difficulty, yet ready to be challenged and excited for the growth and achievement to come. When you truly believe that you can change and become a better version of yourself, then you are willing to venture out into unknown territory. Your comfort zone is no longer a cage that holds you, but a home base that sends you. You may not love change, but you're willing to pursue it for the prize of making progress.

***Your comfort zone is no longer a cage that holds you, but a home base that sends you.***

At this point you may be thinking, "Great, I have a fixed mindset. Now what?" The good new is, you're not doomed to stay there. Dweck discovered she could help school kids by simply teaching them about the growth mindset and that absolutely anyone can get better with practice. By learning that intelligence is not predetermined or set in stone for life, the students began to try harder on tests and assignments and dramatically improved their grades. They just needed to hear the truth.

Here's the key: your success or failure begins with your mindset. If you believe that people don't change, then you won't try or you'll find ways to sabotage yourself. Every effort to change requires that you first believe it's possible. For that to happen, you need a growth mindset.

Perhaps you have reached this point and decided you have a growth mindset. Are you sure? According to Dweck, just because you believe you can grow in one area of your life doesn't mean you believe the same is possible for other areas. You may practice your musical instrument every day, but when it comes to math, you think there is just no hope. Or you could love math, but assume there is no way you will ever overcome your shyness. In both cases you pursue growth in one area, but feel fixed in another.

Our culture has led us down this path by celebrating prodigies and highly skilled people. We assume that experts in any field are born with incredible, if not supernatural, amounts of talent. While I would never discredit natural ability, many high performers would not consider themselves naturally great. The truth is that they invest thousands of hours in private and deliberate practice before they become publically acclaimed.

In *Talent is Overrated*, author Geoff Colvin asserts that "intelligence is a process, not a thing." We choose to become great through hard work, not simply because we were born that way. The talent myth discourages most people from ever putting their all into their dream. Just because you aren't wealthy, healthy or madly in love right now doesn't mean you can't get there. When we fail to see the process that those we admire have gone through, we assume they have natural abilities that we do not possess. In most areas of life, success has nothing to do with raw talent. It does, however, have everything to do with purpose, passion and practice. All of which begins with a growth mindset.

***Just because you aren't wealthy, healthy or madly in love right now doesn't mean you can't get there.***

**Mindset #2: Abundance vs. Scarcity**

We all live somewhere in the spectrum between abundance and scarcity thinking. Whenever you want to do something new, you need the resources to do it. The position you take between these two mindsets defines the quantity and quality of resources that you believe are at your disposal.

You can view the world as plentiful and full of opportunity, or as dangerous and limited, where only a few survive. Unfortunately, most of us live closer to the latter reality. Regardless of what is actually available to us, we can only use what we see and we only see what we believe exists.

***We can only use what we see and we only see what we believe exists.***

I'm not referring to the abundance or scarcity of just finances and possessions, but rather that of resources and possibilities. When you set a goal worth attaining, there's a good chance that you will need some help. You may need to find the right people, food, tools, education, time or investment capital. If it seems like nothing and no one is available to you, then you risk giving up before you even start.

In order to believe that your goal is possible, you have to see the world as abundant, with a place that only you can fill. A scarcity mindset sees the world as a plate of food with a limited number of bites. If someone else has what you need, or is doing what you want to do, then there is nothing left for you. Scarcity tries to convince you that what you want isn't even available, so you should just give up.

Perhaps you want to advance your career, but assume there are no openings in your company or any other. Or you may wish to be a life coach but wonder how you could possibly offer value to people that they can't already find at a seminar or in a book. If you believe that your dream has a no-vacancy sign up, then it's unlikely you will ever try knocking.

When we get stuck in the scarcity mindset of "there's not enough out there for me", we stop trying. When we don't seek, knock or ask for more, we will never find, discover or receive and the cycle of scarcity perpetuates itself. This restrictive mindset has the power to stop us dead in our tracks. Its basic nature is a belief that what we have is all there is, and that what we want is limited by forces outside of our control.

***When we don't seek, knock or ask for more, the cycle of scarcity perpetuates itself.***

Your deepest desires are possible. Whether you need finances, coaches, friends, information or wisdom, they are not outside of your reach forever. They are available to you if you will step outside of your current thinking. It's time to stop staring at the problem and start looking towards the solution. Believe that there is more for you in this life and that what you have now is just the beginning. Where you are going is fully possible by God's grace and your courageous action.

### Mindset #3: Cause and Effect vs. Fate

Life is always in motion, moving towards something. Every choice you make puts you on a path that goes in one direction or another, whether positive or negative. The results you're experiencing today may have to do with weight, body shape, finances, relationships or career, but regardless of what it is, you are here because of steps in this direction. Those steps may have seemed small at the time, like having a cookie and a coffee every afternoon, or going out for dinner every night, but they have added up to a state in which you are not happy to remain.

It's not your fate to be where you don't want to be. Rather, it is cause and effect in action. A prime example is in the debate of Lifestyle versus Genetics. Some believe that genetics are what determine everything about our lives. According to their advocates, our genes have the power to say we will be smart, thin and healthy or dumb, fat and sick. However, other experts would agree in their ability to shape our lives, but would add an important factor.

Dr. Bruce Lipton is a biologist and advocate of lifestyle over genetics. In his book, *The Biology of Belief*, he explains that a protein sheath covers our DNA. Behind it, our genes lay dormant, ready and waiting for action. This sheath is covered with receptors that are constantly monitoring the cell's environment, waiting for instructions on what to do next. As lifestyle factors, like diet and exercise, change the cell's environment, different parts of the protein sheath open up.

When different genes along your DNA are exposed, they express themselves and produce some kind of a result in your body. According to Lipton, that means you can be genetically predisposed to a disease, but you would never suffer from it if you lived in a way that prevented its expression. Your genes play a powerful role in your life and health. While not every problem or disease can be avoided, you do have a measure of choice in the matter.

We are not merely the products of fate, forced to sit back and take whatever life sends our way. Many believe that everything happens on purpose and that where we are is exactly where we should be. This type of thinking feels good because it removes our responsibility and gives us the permission to avoid taking action. However, if life is largely influenced by cause and effect, then everything does happen for a reason, but not everything HAS to happen.

***Everything happens for a reason, but not everything HAS to happen.***

Even God's perfect plan isn't a guarantee. How many people have felt like God made a promise to them, but then it never came to fruition? Destiny is a final destination that God wants to help us reach, but it's up to us to live in the right direction by making the right choices.

When you believe that everything in your life is supposed to be there, you settle and allow it to remain. When you accept your role as co-creator in your own life, the true abundant purposes of God are finally given the opportunity to enter. God wants unbelievably great things for you, but it requires partnership.

There is nothing wrong with waiting on God to tell you what

to do next. In fact, it's very wise. However, there comes a time to stop waiting, because He has no interest in doing it for you.

As you adopt the worldview of cause and effect, you can finally get excited about your opportunity for breakthrough. God hasn't done this to you, He hasn't chosen it to teach you a lesson and He certainly doesn't want you to remain stuck in a painful place. As you begin to do things differently, everything can and will change. Are you ready to believe it?

## Worldview Type 2: THE NATURE OF LIFE

*The Nature of Life* is the way you define the many different people, places and things within the world. Where *The Way It Is* worldview is what we accept as universal laws that we can't change, *The Nature of Life* worldview is how we expect the many parts of life to function. It is both how we perceive things are, as well as how we think they should be.

These beliefs are the standards to which we hold ourselves and other people. Our positive meanings create a promise of pleasure and gain that draws us into action. Negativity, on the other hand, is a natural repellent. When we criticize people or what they represent, we make a secret commitment to avoid whatever might make us like them. How can your heart let you become someone you don't like?

As we go through examples of common beliefs, be willing to see and examine your own. A problem with breakthrough might be a case of your brain trying to protect you from something you said you don't like. Remember, we aren't always logical. When a life circumstance brings us close to something "dangerous" or "evil", it produces a negative feeling. This discomfort wants to trigger an action, albeit self-sabotaging, to keep us safe and secure.

## The Nature of People

The Nature of People is what you believe about specific individuals or groups of people in your life. Based on what you assume about others and the kind of relationship you want to have with them, you choose how you're going to live. If you want to be like them or get close to them, then your actions will mimic theirs and you will do what you can to meet their expectations. If you want nothing to do with them, then you will feel a natural pull in the opposite direction.

When I was young, I knew a girl who seemed to suddenly begin to struggle with bulimia. I learned years later that it began after overhearing a conversation between her father and his friend. Her father had recently broken up with his girlfriend and said that her weight played a factor in his decision. Through the mind of a child, this young girl believed that her father wouldn't love her if she were fat. Her conclusion was to never gain weight and she went to extreme measures to accomplish it. In her mind, it was to maintain her father's love.

We all find ways to fit with what we assume to be true about other people. We define them in our own minds and then make an assumption about what they expect from us. From those assumptions, we then choose to live either towards them or away from them.

***We all find ways to fit with what we assume to be true about other people.***

| People Worldview | The Outcome |
| --- | --- |
| God only cares about my spiritual health. | This person may choose to completely neglect physical, mental and emotional health in order to please God with great spirituality. Any attempt to focus on these other life areas may feel both meaningless and unpleasing to God. |
| My father and mother love me when I succeed. | This person might only do the things that guarantee success and steer clear of anything that carries the risk of failure. When new opportunities arise, they are quickly dismissed and God's best is never realized. Why? Because saying "no" is easier than the thought of failing and losing the love and acceptance of others. |
| My brother/sister is the smart one of the family. | In order to fit within the family, this person may try to be the athletic or the popular one, always carrying the identity of "the dumb one". As a result, any time a life challenge comes that requires a lot of thought and intelligence, the default is to give up and let "whatever happens happen". |
| Overweight people are happy and well-liked. | This person may believe that if the weight goes away, so do all the friends. In order to remain safely within the current group, one must continually sabotage all weight loss attempts. |
| Rich people are stuck up and selfish. | A person trying to gain financial freedom will be quickly stopped by this belief. In order to be compassionate and loving, how can there possibly be an accumulation of wealth? |

| People Worldview | The Outcome |
|---|---|
| Women/men are always trying to control you. | A young person who always feels controlled by mom or dad may expect the same to happen in every relationship. As a result, there comes an assumed choice between two unhealthy extremes: to submit and be passive, or take control and dominate. |
| Suzy is always judging me. | Whenever this person sees Suzy, or anyone else with a negative impression, a sudden sense of discomfort and moodiness kicks in. |
| Only people over 30 are taken seriously. | This person may never try to step out of the norm to be different. Instead it is safer to sit back and let life happen until thirty comes, because no one will take notice anyways. |

## The Nature of Roles

As you learned in the Values chapter, we live a multitude of roles. It might be father, mother, son, daughter, teacher, student, manager, employee, athlete, painter or a hundred other things. Whatever roles you happen to be living right now are partially or fully defined by your own mind.

The Nature of Roles will cause problems in three ways. The first is when your expectations are not met. For example, you have a definition for what makes a good father or mother. If your spouse or your parents aren't living up to those standards by doing what you think is required, you can become frustrated or judgmental and feel short-changed.

The second problem occurs when change requires compromise. You may have a clear idea of how to raise your children. But what if you can't give them everything they want anymore, and that is the best way you have learned to love them? When an effort to change seems to require that you compromise on your definition of a "good parent," or any other role, then you have been set up to fail before you begin.

Finally, the third problem enters in when change is going to expose some kind of inadequacy. If you believe that doing something new, like taking a promotion and becoming a manager, will expose you as a fraud, you're likely to limit yourself.

In order to prevent these three problems from damaging our relationships and change efforts, we must understand our roles worldview.

| Role Worldview | The Outcome |
|---|---|
| A leader should always have all the answers. | A belief like this can make an employee critical of his boss's mistakes, or make a manager afraid to act. |
| A good father gives his children what they want. | This can make a man feel inadequate if he doesn't earn enough money to pay for everything his kids want. He can also feel badly about cutting back on spending to meet financial goals. |
| A mother should always put her needs last. | If a mother is trying to get healthy, it may require that she set aside time for herself. Believing that she is depriving her family of what they deserve can put her right back into her old habits, moving away from her new goal. |

| Role Worldview | The Outcome |
|---|---|
| A husband should always make more money than his wife. | This could prevent a man from quitting his job and starting his own business or cause resentment if his wife has a higher income. |
| An athlete does whatever it takes to win. | All competitive athletes want to win, but those who are willing to do anything can get into trouble with legal and ethical issues. Choosing to set up boundaries is smart, but it can make them feel like failures in their sport. |
| A good employee should never make a mistake. | Many people believe that making a mistake is a sign of failure. This person may be afraid to try something new for fear that it will show an inability to perform. The result of this risk-aversion is precisely what was feared in the first place—failure. |
| A good friend should never say no to a request. | People-pleasers have a hard time saying no to a request, afraid that it might compromise their relationships. If new choices are getting in the way of the desires of others, this person may give up on his or her change efforts. |
| A good son/daughter always does what his/her parents want. | This belief can cause a parent to resent a child when there is conflict or rebellion. It can also make it difficult for a man or woman to establish boundaries around his or her family when it comes to the needs and desires of parents. |

## The Nature of Places

Thoughts, emotions and habits are often closely linked to places. In a never-ending pursuit of efficiency, your brain connects your physical location with whatever you think, feel or do most while you are there. Now whenever you reenter those places, the same old thoughts, emotions and habits are quickly triggered and ready to serve (or hurt) you.

The places we go and the people we find there have a significant influence on our mental and emotional states. It might be that you feel uncontrollable cravings whenever you walk into your kitchen. It has been a place of overindulgence for so long that the physical location takes you back to that feeling, which then takes you back into the habitual act of eating. Whatever your self-sabotaging behaviours may be, if you do them in the same place enough times, then that place can become a trigger point for more of the same.

| **Place Worldview** | **The Outcome** |
|---|---|
| School is boring and useless. | This person, even as an adult, will disengage and drift off whenever in a place of learning. |
| The gym is full of meatheads showing off. | A person with this perception will avoid the gym, expecting to feel judged immediately upon walking through the door. |
| The kitchen is where I give in to cravings. | Every time this person walks into the room, an uncontrollable urge to eat seems to take over. |
| Church is full of hypocrites. | A past hurt involving people in the church can make it difficult to go into a church building without feeling uneasy. |
| Work is where I fail. | Those who feel inadequate in what they do can feel intense stress every time they walk in the door. They may also avoid the tough decisions or projects that could be an opportunity for career advancement. |

| Place Worldview | The Outcome |
| --- | --- |
| Going home means having another fight. | This person may choose to stay late at work to avoid going home. And when it is time to go home, the emotional guard goes up and it feels impossible to connect. |

## The Nature of Times

Similar to physical location, our emotions and thoughts can link up with specific times of the day or year. It might be the habit of eating something sweet every day at 3pm or the feeling of sadness for a week surrounding the anniversary of the loss of a loved one. The bottom line is that our feelings flow with times and seasons and if we are unaware, we can just accept them and allow them to lead our lives.

| Time Worldview | The Outcome |
| --- | --- |
| Mondays are evil. | Many people spend their entire Sunday evening dreading work on Monday morning. |
| Christmas is a time for family to be together. | What if the person who believes this has a sibling that spends the holidays somewhere else? It can cause serious disappointment and stress on the relationship. |
| Weekends are for relaxing. | These people might have a lot of trouble getting to work on their side projects. Although they want financial freedom, they also don't want to lose the only free time they have. Instead, they give in to the temptation of watching movies, playing games and just hanging out. |

## The Nature of Ideas

Everything related to the success of your goal has its own definition. A goal of financial independence, for example, involves beliefs about money, work and status, among other things. The way you think about each one can heavily influence your ability to accept the victory as part of your life.

***Everything related to the success of your goal has its own definition.***

As I mentioned earlier, the things you celebrate, or at least appreciate, are let in, while the things you criticize are kept out. It is critical that you understand what your heart is saying about the things you are trying to achieve. You may want something badly, but if that thing connects with what you secretly want to avoid, your heart will wear you out until you give up and give in to the status quo.

| Idea Worldview | The Outcome |
|---|---|
| Life should always be fair. | As soon as life produces an unfair result, this person just wants to quit. We live in an imperfect world and while we can be deliberate and wise, we do need to endure unfair circumstances on the road to our goals. |
| Money is the root of evil. | This person, even with a strong desire for financial freedom, will secretly stay away from any amount of abundance in that area. |

| Idea Worldview | The Outcome |
|---|---|
| There is never enough time. | This person can feel overwhelmed by life, not taking action because it will just be another thing that won't get done in the end. |
| Success is having everything I want. | This belief can make life stressful, always striving for bigger and better things. It can make it nearly impossible to save for the future because delaying gratification feels like delaying success. |
| Beauty is tall and skinny. | People with this belief may not want to try improving their physical health and shape, assuming they can never really be beautiful if they don't meet those criteria. |
| Love is doing nice things. | Someone who wants a deeper marriage may think that nice acts is the greatest sign of love. However, his or her mate may receive love in a different way. |
| Holidays are for people who aren't fully committed. | This person may not take a much-needed break, which eventually leads to burnout, poor health and serious mistakes. |
| Taking breaks will make me less successful. | Those who believe this may want to lose weight, but then go all day without eating because that requires taking breaks. As a result, their metabolism slows down and they overeat at night, which leads to weight gain and a big challenge with losing it. |

**Up Next**

The first three stories all culminate at the fourth. The pathways of your brain and life are what ultimately drive your impulses, cravings and choices. Now it's time to dive into the world of your invisible commitments and their power over your future.

# CHAPTER 5
# THE FOURTH STORY: PATHWAYS - HOW I MUST LIVE

*To their friends and family, Andrew and Katelyn seemed to be careless spenders. Andrew always had to have the latest gadget and Katelyn had piles of clothes she had hardly worn once. While they both said they wanted to pay down debt, plan for the future and eventually become financially free, their constant spending prevented them from making any meaningful headway towards those goals.*

*Like many young girls, Katelyn grew up learning that women must meet society's definition of beauty to have success and worth in the world. Although She had matured over the years and was able to confidently say that beauty comes in many ways, one habit she couldn't seem to kick was shopping. Katelyn's brain made an advertising-induced association between fashion and beauty, which seemed to tell her that to be beautiful, one must also be "fashionable."*

*Her husband, Andrew, grew up without a lot. Both of his parents worked hard just to keep the family fed and cared for. Andrew's childhood best friend, on the other hand, always seemed to have the newest toys. While he never felt jealous of his friend, Andrew decided early on that true success meant he and his family would always have whatever they wanted.*

*For both Andrew and Katelyn, status was a driving force behind their spending habits. When a new phone came out, or a close friend was wearing the latest fashion, they felt like they were missing out. It seemed as though they weren't successful or beautiful enough if they didn't also have those things.*

*To make matters worse, shopping had become a habitual form of therapy for the both of them. Whenever they felt down, buying something new created a sense of pleasure at a time when nothing else seemed to do the trick. The perpetual feeling of inadequacy that both Andrew and Katelyn felt caused the two of them to spend their money excessively when every other part of them desperately wanted to save. While their eyes were set on financial freedom, their hearts and brains had other plans.*

---

We all live by our own unique set of neural pathways in the brain. These connections form to create habitual ways of feeling, thinking and doing. This gives our conscious minds some space to focus on the present moment while the rest of our lives are managed for us.

Unfortunately, our pathways often create impulses that confuse us. They influence our choices and promote decisions that feel critical in the moment, but cause regret once we have time to look back and think about them. The fear, anxiety, frustration, apathy, anger, and a whole host of other negative feelings they create, make us feel like helpless passengers in our own lives.

Why do our pathways sabotage us like this? Believe it or not, it's all in an effort to keep us safe, happy and comfortable.

## Pathways Are For Protection

Do you remember the boy who skinned his knee in chapter one?

He fell from his bike and ran to his father for comfort. The response he received created emotional pain that was greater than his wounded knee, so he determined a new way to live. He set a personal rule to never show emotion again, so that he could gain the respect of others and be a "real" man. This resolution promised to keep him safe from embarrassing himself again and to give him the satisfaction of living like a man.

This kind of scenario can happen in every area of our lives. We all have varying needs for things like power, connection, respect, significance and achievement. When we feel the opposite—powerless, isolated, disrespected, insignificant or like a failure—we want to escape the pain. We seek ways to regain what we lost, and our brains create pathways to prevent us from going back to that place of discomfort again in the future.

Stressful situations activate the release of the hormone cortisol and, according to Dr. Loretta Breuning, author of *Meet Your Happy Chemicals*, your brain is quick to respond. First it looks for the source of your problem and then "wires you to recognize these danger cues in the future." To put it simply, when your brain feels bad, it looks for something or someone to blame and then asks, "How can I prevent this from ever happening again?" In our case above, the boy is now on a constant lookout for opportunities where he may become too emotional.

***When your brain feels bad, it asks, "How can I prevent this from ever happening again?"***

For someone else, it could mean becoming aggressive in the workplace in order to feel respected and significant. Another may give in to all the demands of other people so to not feel rejected and alone. A third might become a control freak to avoid failure caused by the mistakes of other people. When we feel upset, stressed out or in crisis, the perceived cause of our pain becomes a new enemy to avoid at all costs.

Thankfully, our protective pathways can also produce a positive result. For example, someone who never had an interest in healthy living can make a radical change after a family member dies of a preventable disease. Another person learns the value of diligent practice and preparation after an embarrassingly poor performance in the classroom, on stage or at home. Pain, therefore, has the power to create both supportive and unsupportive pathways.

***Pain has the power to create both supportive and unsupportive pathways.***

### Pathways Are For Pleasure

On the other end of the spectrum, Dr. Breuning writes, "when something changes unhappy chemicals [cortisol] to happy chemicals, your brain learns from the experience." In pathways for protection, your brain learns the cause of pain and seeks to avoid it in the future. In pathways for pleasure, on the other hand, it takes note of what stopped pain, created pleasure or a combination of both, and seeks to reproduce those situations or behaviours as often as possible.

When the injured boy stopped crying, he felt as though he had earned his father's respect, so he could feel good again. In that moment, his young brain assumes that the same action (avoiding emotion) will always produce the same pleasure of love and respect. As a result, a neural pathway is formed.

When we find a source of what we value—strength, respect,

acceptance, adventure, achievement, or whatever else is important or pleasurable to us—our brains remember. In an effort to keep going back to that feeling in the future, a pathway forms to reproduce the same behaviours that we assume took us there in the first place.

***To keep going back to that feeling in the future, a pathway forms to reproduce the same behaviours.***

For one person, it could be going for a run, spending time with friends or feeding the homeless. For another, it may be eating junk food, having a drink or spending the evening in front of the television. Your choice behaviours, whatever they may be, become impulsive and irresistible cravings as your brain chases after more good feelings.

These pathways to pleasure, however, don't just come from past experience. They also develop from expectations. Our culture, for instance, promises that making more money, driving the right cars and having certain types of relationships will all make us happy and fulfilled. As a result, we can compromise our health, waste our money and ruin our relationships, all in an effort to attain an empty promise. If financial stability means you will lose out on the many purchases that will make you feel fulfilled, which commitment do you think will win? Whatever we secretly believe will create a positive experience, both now and in the future, has the power to become our committed way of life.

## Pathways Are For Comfort & Convenience

Our brains learn and automate, but it's not always about pain and pleasure. The simple act of doing something over and over makes it easier and more natural as habits begin to form. Our habits allow us to drive a car, brush our teeth or walk down the street while thinking about something else. They automate common behaviours so we can move on to more important things.

Our daily rituals feel comfortable and easy because they travel down well-paved neural pathways. Try to take a step off that easy road, like stopping at the gym when you always go straight home after work, and you feel a little uneasy. A war begins to wage inside of you, trying to push you back to your habit and away from that thing that just doesn't "feel right."

Your brain fights to protect your pathways. It believes that change will open the door to pain, shut you off from pleasure and put your life in danger. You secretly assume that your current pathways are the safest and surest way to live, because it's all you really know.

***You secrety assume that your current pathways are the safest and surest way to live.***

Breaking a habit requires that you step off your well-worn pathway and start moving in a new direction. Your brain perceives this as a threat to your very survival, so it goes on the defense by making you feel anxious, frustrated and afraid. Although the danger feels real, it's simply a chemical reaction inside your brain, designed to push you back to what feels comfortable, convenient and safe.

## Pathways From Stories

As we develop each new identity, value and worldview story, we turn it into an action statement that operates much like a personal life rule. First is identity. If you learn as a child that you are of little worth (identity) and feel most accepted when helping others (pleasure pathway), it becomes natural to commit to always compromising personal desires for the sake of other people. A young woman may believe she is ugly (identity) and determine that she will never leave the house without makeup (pain pathway). In essence, we find ways to prevent pain and increase pleasure in light of what we believe about ourselves.

***We find ways to prevent pain and increase pleasure in light of what we believe about ourselves.***

When it comes to values, two different people can learn to value helpfulness and hard work as children. However, based on different experiences or life lessons, one might live those values by doing work alongside other people, while the other learns to simply do everyone's work for them. At the same time we learn a value, we create a pathway for how to express it.

***At the same time we learn a value, we create a pathway for how to express it.***

I remember a time as a young teen when my dad was digging a hole in the backyard while I just stood there watching. After only a few minutes, he looked up at me and said, "Matthew, you should always take initiative in life and look for opportunities to help others." I felt embarrassed for just standing there and, to this day, I still feel foolish whenever someone else is working hard and I am not. It is a value pathway that has served me well.

Finally comes your worldview, where you choose a specific path to get to the life you want. For example, if your worldview says that fate determines your life, then you might create an anti-pain pathway by committing to always accept, "whatever will be, will be." With this rule, you will never get hurt by trying and failing because you "know" that what you have is what you SHOULD have. A worldview sets the terrain and your pathways form around the perceived obstacles.

***A worldview sets the terrain and your pathways form around the perceived obstacles.***

In summary, your identity says who you are, your values determine what is most important, your worldview paints a map of the world and your pathways try to keep you living safely and congruently within them all. Each one of the first three stories has been secretly converted into rules so that you will always stay true to your heart.

## The Pathway Types

Now that we have covered the pathway sources, let's take a look at the types. While largely invisible and unspoken, they function as stories that can be clearly defined.

### *Pathway Type 1: MY PERSONAL PROMISE*

*My Personal Promise* pathways are governing black and white rules for your life. They are absolutes that begin with "Always" and "Never". When you act against them, you feel uncomfortable and unsafe, so you move back into your comfort zone and your familiar self-sabotaging choices.

Some examples of My Personal Promise include:

- To always be thin.
- To never be mean to my kids.
- To never get in the way.
- To never look foolish.
- To always appear calm and collected.
- To never be disrespected.
- To always be nice.
- To always be loved and admired.
- To never fail.
- To never have too much.
- To always get what I want.
- To always get love in whatever way I can.

*Pathway Type 2: MY WAY TO SUCCESS*

*My Way to Success* pathways are similar to *My Personal Promises*, but offer more insight into their purpose. They exist to protect you from what you fear, and to help satisfy your needs and desires. Whether to guard you from inadequacy, rejection, and loss, or to experience achievement, acceptance and control, they are personal guarantees that put up a good fight against any threat.

These types of pathways are equations of what action will produce the result you want, and can be expressed with If/Then statements. According to Dr. Milton Cudney and Robert Hardy, authors of *Self-Defeating Behaviors*, beliefs like these describe the "unconscious bargain that you've made with yourself to avoid growth and change." So although you may not believe these declarations logically, they make an emotional promise that is nearly impossible to explain away.

Examples of My Way to Success include:

- If I get my way, then no one can take advantage of me.
- If I don't cry, then others will respect me.
- If I defer my authority, then I won't be exposed as a bad leader.
- If I don't open up, then I won't be exploited or abused.
- If I keep my thoughts to myself, then I can't be wrong.
- If I don't trust others, then I will never be disappointed.
- If I worry, then bad things won't happen to me.
- If I have fewer possessions than other people, then I will be accepted and loved.

### *Pathway Type 3: MY AUTOMATIC ACTIONS*

*My Automatic Actions* are exactly as they sound: prescheduled behaviours that happen without thinking. They can be triggered by time, location, sound, smell, emotion, another person or a thing in your environment, just to name a few. While the first two pathways point to the outcome you want, this one describes what you will do to get there. We believe these actions will protect us from pain, produce a reward or make life easier through habit. When the behaviour is called upon, you feel an irresistible urge to act. If you attempt to resist the habit, your automatic pathway tries to manipulate you with feelings of irritability and anxiety.

These pathways are inactive until their corresponding triggers turn them on. As such, we can define them with "When/I Will" statements. They're just waiting for their chance to get off the bench and into the game.

Your automatic actions come from two places. First, they can flow directly out of the other pathways. In these cases, general rules receive practical application. For example, "If I don't speak up, then I can't be wrong" creates, "When in a group setting, I will sit as far away from the main talkers as possible." Now when you walk into a meeting, you feel uncomfortable if the only seat left is beside the chairperson.

The second source is through repetition. These are habitual pathways that form over time and stand on their own. Although they don't appear to serve a deeper purpose, they are just as strong in their ability to influence our lives.

| Automatic Action | Related Pathway |
|---|---|
| When my child throws a tantrum, I will give him/her what he/she wants. | To never be mean to my kids. |
| When my savings reaches $1,000, I will go shopping. | To never have too much. |
| When I am hurt, I will be quiet. | To never get in the way. |
| When I don't get what I want, I will start shouting. | If I get my way, then no one can take advantage of me. |
| When emotions get high, I will disappear for a while. | If I don't cry, then others will respect me. |
| When I see David, I will feel anxious and act aggressively. | If I attack, then attackers can't hurt me. |
| When there is food on my plate, I will eat it all. | To never be wasteful. |
| When I feel sad, I will go shopping. | None |
| When I get home from work, I will watch TV and have a drink. | None |
| When 4pm comes, I will eat something sweet. | None |

## From Stories to Pathways

For a better idea of how stories become pathways, let's look at a few examples.

Identity to Pathway:

| Identity Story | Pathway |
|---|---|
| I am dumb. | To never speak up. |
| I am worthless. | If I never say no, then others will love me. |
| I am not the kind of person who makes good decisions. | To always defer my authority. |
| I am not athletic. | If I don't try to be physically active, then I won't look foolish. |

Value to Pathway:

| Value Story | Pathway |
|---|---|
| Achievement | If I don't take vacations, then I will get more done. |
| Acceptance | To always do what other people want. |
| Safety | If I stay overweight, then I won't have to deal with sexual advances. |
| Love | To always accept love in whatever way it is given. |

Worldview to Pathway:

| Worldview Story | Pathway |
|---|---|
| Beauty is tall and skinny. | To never gain weight. |
| Intelligence is set at birth. | If I don't try, then I won't fail. |
| Life doesn't tolerate weakness. | To always appear strong. |
| People take advantage of each other. | If I push others away, then they can't hurt me. |

Any goal to change your life in some way will include one or more new pathways. Whether to eat certain foods, spend less money or communicate more effectively, you need to act differently. When your new commitments meet opposing pathways, your best intentions lose almost every time. The secret then, is to pave new pathways.

**Up Next**

Now that you have a better understanding of the four core stories, it's time to set your sights on changing them. Part two of getting free to change is about uncovering the truth, which all begins with vision.

# PART 2
# EDIT YOUR STORIES

# Chapter 6
# Crafting a Powerful Vision

What would happen if your immune system lost sight of good health?

When your body gets sick, it goes on a quest to find and destroy the enemy, and bring you back into balance. However, if this God-given wisdom is disrupted, your immune system can switch from friend to foe and start waging war on you.

This is what happens with an autoimmune disease. Your immune system starts working abnormally, producing antibodies that attack your body instead of the invaders. It becomes "confused" about the end goal and starts working against the natural design of good health. Similar to an immune system without the right image of health, a life without vision is full of actions and beliefs that steal from your potential.

A lasting transformation can't happen without the right stories, which first require a new picture. Your mind stores every memory and belief as a series of images with a narrative. Whether you believe yourself to be strong, weak, beautiful or ugly, each one is playing on the stage of your imagination.

Try it for yourself. What does it mean for you to be strong? Or weak? What about beautiful or ugly? I'm willing to bet that your mind called up pictures to answer those questions. We are such visual thinkers that all of our stories function at an image level.

If your limiting identity, values, worldviews and pathways are an accumulation of little pictures, then new pictures can play a powerful role in the process of inspiring and driving change. This is where vision comes in.

## Vision Is Purposeful

Imagine building your own home. You don't begin with a shovel in-hand. You start by researching and imagining all of the wonderful features and options your dream home will offer. You envision the kitchen and see the stainless steel appliances, the marble countertops, the large center island and the big beautiful windows that flood the room with natural light. You go through the house in your mind's eye and see the shape and size of each room, how they connect and flow, and how each room is furnished.

Then comes the architect to help finish your vision and create the drawings and blueprints. You must decide the location of every wall, the height of every ceiling and a place for every appliance, so that every part of the build is on purpose. First you envision, then you plan and then you execute.

If your contractor and tradespeople have no direction or vision, they won't know what to build or where to build it. If everyone showed up and started doing whatever seemed right to him or her, there would be no order or structure. You would have to hope and pray that something resembling a livable house would come out of their chaotic efforts, but there would be no guarantee.

Although we can agree that it makes no sense to build a house without a blueprint, many of us make a worse mistake and live our lives without one. Too many people wake up every day not knowing what they are living and working towards. They know they aren't happy, but they have no idea what will make life better or how to start moving in the right direction.

If success is going to stick in our lives, we need to set our stories and our actions on a common purpose. That happens through vision.

***If success is going to stick, we need to set our stories and our actions on a common purpose.***

## Vision is the End

Vision creates a positive picture of the future. In his hugely successful book, *The 7 Habits of Highly Effective People*, author Stephen Covey outlines what he believes to be the major principles of success, learned through his study of the lives of successful people. In habit number two, Covey explains that we must "begin with the end in mind." In other words, we need to look into the future and determine the final result before we start to move in any direction.

One of the most famous and compelling examples of the power of vision was seen in the life and work of Walt Disney. Disney was a master of vision. He once said, "I first saw the site for Disneyland back in 1953. In those days it was all flat land—no rivers, no mountains, no castles or rocket ships—just orange groves, and a few acres of walnut trees." With vision, Disney was able to fully imagine and see his creations long before they were ever built.

Living without vision is like driving without a destination or building without a blueprint. We feel busy doing lots of different things, but we're not actually being productive, nor do we arrive at a meaningful destination.

## Vision Leads

Life is always in motion and we are always moving in one direction or another. Because movement is inevitable, the more we become complacent or try to wing it as we go, the further we fall behind. Instead, we must become co-leaders in our own lives and set a direction for the way we want to go.

One of the first lessons I remember learning in driving school was how to escape a problem situation. Whether you are skidding sideways, heading towards a ditch or trying to avoid an oncoming vehicle, the instructor was adamant that you must only look straight ahead (to where you want to go) as you attempt to regain control. He explained that wherever you look, your car will follow. Your eyes naturally lead your hands, and if you look to the ditch or at oncoming headlights, that's precisely where you will go.

This same principle holds true in our daily lives, as the objects of our focus pull us in the direction of our gaze. If all you focus on is your weight, your overspending, your anger or your insecurity, all you will get is more of the same. Remember the Reticular Activating System and Confirmation Bias? They are working hard every day to keep you seeing, believing and producing the same results.

***The objects of our focus pull us in the direction of our gaze.***

Rather than staring at your problems, positive vision lifts your focus to the God-given potential within you, so that you can overcome your current circumstances. You have the ability to choose your destination and then start moving in the direction that will take you there. Vision becomes a clear standard, a way to measure success and a target to approach.

## Vision Aligns

Vision, because of its size and power, gives our identity, values, worldview, pathways and actions something to gather around. It provides a standard to weigh what we believe and to choose something more truthful and empowering.

We live inside of invisible walls, built by the beliefs we assume to be true. Because we can't always see them, it's difficult to identify what may be out of order. Plus, when truth flies in the face of a lie we currently believe, we are quick to reject it. As a result, we have a hard time figuring out what to believe. Vision makes it easier, though, because it asks a better question.

***Vision asks a better question.***

Try to write a more empowering story without vision and all you think to ask is, "What's the truth?" But without a context, this open-ended question is nearly impossible to answer. Pose it to the next person you see and the answer will likely be, "The truth about what?"

Attempting to change your stories without the clarity of vision is like standing in front of a store shelf with hundreds of options. They may all be good, but which ones are great? What exact stories do you need in order to truly move forward? Vision helps answer these questions by asking, "What do I need to believe in order for this end result to be possible?"

For example:

- "What do I need to believe about myself to finish the big project on time?"
- "What do I need to value most in order to lose 100 pounds?"
- "What must be true about the world for my marriage to be restored?"
- "What must I commit to in order to generate $2 million in revenue per month?"

Vision has the power to both expose the lies and to organize our truthful and empowering stories to point in the right direction. As that alignment takes place, life begins to produce results with far greater ease.

Here is an example of story alignment for a vision of great physical health.

> **Identity:** I'm the kind of person who commits to his/her word and follows through.
>
> **Value:** Better health will help me satisfy my love for family and need for achievement.
>
> **Worldview:** Life is cause and effect.
>
> **Pathway:** If I make healthy choices, then I will be an inspiration to others.

As you can see, all of your stories must support your vision and make it possible. Each category would typically have multiple stories, but this gives you an idea of how everything can point in a single direction.

## Vision is Bigger Than Problems

Life is full of obstacles and hard times that have the potential to take us out of the game. When something appears to be too big to overcome, we give up. How do we become so overwhelmed by the size of our problems? It happens when we lack vision.

An obstacle that stands in the way of your success can be small or big, but its ultimate impact depends on how you see it. A little problem can shake the ground beneath you and a time of utter chaos can be totally manageable. It all comes down to perspective.

Change may require the discomfort of addressing your feelings with a loved one to clear the air and move on to a better relationship. You might need to cut out some of your favourite foods because they're preventing weight loss. Or perhaps you have to resist the new car or extravagant vacation to keep your retirement plan on track. Whatever it is you need to do can seem impossible and unfair if you don't see it in the right way. Spilled milk really is worth crying over when it's all you think you have in life.

***Spilled milk really is worth crying over when it's all you think you have in life.***

Vision puts your challenges in perspective by placing them in comparison to the mountain of success that you're approaching. Facing a little bit of pain isn't so bad when you clearly see the joy and victory of your future. The Bible says that Jesus endured the pain of the cross "for the joy set before Him" (Hebrews 12:2). Did He want to die? Absolutely not! But He was willing, because He could see the vision of its purpose. When you are willing and able to look up to see what God sees and believe what He believes, everything else seems more temporary and manageable.

## Vision is Compelling

Emotion is an essential component of change. We discussed the power of WHY in the Values chapter as well as how logical goal setting has no longevity when it doesn't feel meaningful. We all need something to obsess over. Something that will capture and hold our attention day by day. What we focus on and get emotional about is what determines our final destination, so unless we are compelled by a great vision, our goals will never stick.

***What we focus on and get emotional about is what determines our final destination.***

There is a multitude of books on the subject of goals from how to set them to how to measure and achieve them. The majority of this content isn't wrong, but unless you have real passion behind your goals, even the most well-intentioned ambitions won't help you. Goals frame your house, but they need to be set on the foundation of purpose and passion to be successful.

You can say that you want to lose 30 pounds, but if you don't feel emotional about it, then it won't stick and you likely won't lose the weight. However, all is not lost if you don't yet feel it. You have the power to develop an emotional connection with your goal by experiencing it with vision before it ever happens.

Vision is a bright, positive and exciting future that makes you feel alive. You were made for something great, so you get excited when you see it! But when vision is lost, passion dries up and you forget about what's possible. Instead of advancing to something bigger and better, you settle for the small thing you already have.

## Vision Creates Tension

A big part of why vision is so compelling is the tension it creates. Just as values activate our inborn desire for justice, vision flips another switch. Whenever you have an ideal scenario in mind, the distance between it and your current circumstances creates a sense of stress. If you feel confident and capable enough to move forward, you become compelled to close that gap and advance your life.

Phil Stutz and Barry Michels, authors of the book *Tools*, have defined this form of tension as jeopardy, which is the fear of losing what you value. There is something inside of us that deeply dislikes loss. It's like the toddler who throws a fit as another child takes the toy he isn't even playing with but thinks belongs to him.

When we possess something, everything inside of us fights to hang on to it. This rule applies to vision as well. Although we have yet to achieve it, if we are emotionally connected enough, we experience a sense of ownership that fights against the possibility of loss.

Whether someone wants you to go shopping and spend the money you're trying to save or you have the desire to sleep in instead of getting up early and going to the gym, the emotional tension caused by jeopardy and the fear of loss will pressure you to make the right choice. But only when vision is big and strong enough.

## Vision Is Huge

In their book, *Built to Last*, authors Jim Collins and Jerry Porras coin what they call, Big Hairy Audacious Goals (BHAGs). Collins and Porras maintain that organizations need to set goals beyond simple tactical and short-term objectives and instead recommend setting "...an audacious 10-to-30-year goal to progress towards an envisioned future." In other words, organizations need big, hairy, audacious goals to increase their likelihood of success and it's easy to argue that we do too.

Short-term and minor goals give you a list of to-do's that help manage and contribute to your progress. Vision and BHAGs, on the other hand, give you something more meaningful and long-term to invest in. They create an opportunity to look into the future and place a demand on yourself to do something that you really care about. BHAGs, therefore, are an important part of your vision. They help inspire you to get up and start moving instead of settling for the comfortable and familiar ways of your present circumstance.

***Look into the future and place a demand on yourself to do something you really care about.***

Vision needs to be huge. It begins with dreaming of the impossible, knowing that nothing is impossible with God. God has a habit of doing far more in us, through us and for us than we can ever hope to wrap our heads around. In 1 Corinthians 2:9 we read, "What no eye has seen, what no ear has heard, and what no human mind has conceived—the things God has prepared for those who love him" (NIV). If God is willing to prepare it, then we need to be willing and courageous enough to imagine it.

***If God is willing to prepare it, then we need to be willing and courageous enough to imagine it.***

Vince Lombardi was a legendary football coach who once said, "The vision is the ideal self the coach believes the player and team are capable of achieving." God has a vision that He wants to give you, and it's huge. It contains everything that He believes you are capable of being and achieving through Christ. If we are able to "do all things through Him who strengthens" us (Philippians 4:13), then His vision of us has no limits.

God sees us as our ideal selves, and He is always willing to do His part. It's up to us to be willing to let Him be our coach. You are capable of more than you think, and if you're honest with yourself, you may agree that you crave something bigger and better for your life. There is something inherent in the human heart that yearns for big dreams, because we have been created by a God who plans big and audacious things.

## Vision is a Partnership

There are times when God will give you the exact vision and direction for an area of your life. He may give a dream or a prophetic word that paints a perfectly clear picture that requires just your faith and action. But that isn't always the case. Many times, He is looking for partners who will tell Him the desires of their own hearts, so that He can support and work with them.

When God completed His creation, He said to Adam and Eve, "Be fruitful and multiply, and fill the earth, and subdue it; and rule over the fish of the sea and over the birds of the sky and over every living thing that moves on the earth" (Genesis 1:28). God created man in His own image, and gave them full control to live out their will on the earth. However, He gave them the choice to act in accordance with His will.

The original design of men and women is one of rulership. He made you to step into life and be fruitful in whatever you do.

He made you for success and He wants to partner with and empower you in whatever you do.

Vision can be big, exciting and effective with or without God's involvement. People use it every day in life and business. But for believers, it becomes all the more powerful when we choose to approach it as a partnership with God.

If it seems like you have no idea what God wants for you, perhaps it's because He is waiting to hear what you want. You're allowed to dream whatever is in your heart. Envision your desires with a heart that loves God and wants to build His kingdom and fulfill His purposes. When this happens, you can trust that your vision will be shaped and molded by Him as you go along. A good rule of thumb to remember is: if your vision fits with God's Word, and improves your life and the lives of other people, you can be confident in moving forward, trusting that He will lead you every step of the way.

## Step Out From Your Past

Vision allows you to see a future that doesn't yet exist. However, you need to first step out from your past and recognize that what happened before doesn't have to be the standard for your future. Everything that has taken place around you, through you and to you has helped shape the person you are today. There is no need to despise your past, because you can never change it. But you *do* need to let it stay there.

Many people fall into the trap of living from their past. Some relive their mistakes and offenses day after day as they consider how bad or cursed they are. Others focus on their glory days and how great things once were, wishing they could go back in time.

In both cases, an unwillingness or inability to take a step out of the past prevents us from seeing and experiencing a great future.

The truth is this: what you focus on is what you experience most. If the pain of your past is all you see, then your life will continue to see and experience that same pain. If, in the light of your glorious past, you focus on how much the quality of your life has declined, then it will continue to go downhill. Like a car, your life follows your line of sight.

Thankfully, God doesn't get stuck in the past. He loves and supports our progress. Throughout history, He has transformed lives and He continues to do it today. Nick Vujicic, for example, is a man who was born with no arms or legs. Despite these obstacles, he travels the world as a motivational speaker and evangelist. He refuses to allow his past experiences or current circumstances to prevent him from living a great life and fulfilling God's purpose.

This story is just one of many human triumphs. Countless instances exist of people overcoming seemingly insurmountable odds and making the past irrelevant in the light of an amazing purpose and future. It doesn't matter where you are now. Good days are ahead of you and God wants you to know that, by partnering with Him, your best days are yet to come.

***By partnering with God, your best days are yet to come.***

Moses entered the most influential phase of his life in his eighties, even though he thought he was finished. Like all of us, his past had mistakes and I can imagine that he lived much of his adult life in regret. Moses went from a position of royalty in his youth to one of a shepherd with low self-esteem, all because of one big lapse in judgment.

When God asked Moses to go to Egypt and rescue His people, Moses replied with, "Please, Lord, I have never been eloquent, neither recently nor in time past, nor since You have spoken to Your servant; for I am slow of speech and slow of tongue" (Exodus 4:10). Moses projected his past and present experience into his future and assumed that nothing else was possible. However, God saw the real Moses hidden under those layers of mistakes and insecurities, and believed in his potential.

Moses became a great leader because he was willing to believe God and take the steps to a new life. Although he made plenty of mistakes along the way, he trusted that God would partner with him and help bring the vision to life. Despite how bad your past or present may be, God wants to do in you the same thing that He did in Moses. He has the desire and the power to pull you up and out of your problems if you will let Him, but it all starts with faith. You must choose to look ahead with fresh eyes, allowing what would seem impossible to become a possibility.

It doesn't matter where you have been, where you are or even what you are capable of doing. Dream without regard for anything but the potential of God in you. When you realize that with God nothing is impossible, you can dream bigger than ever before.

***Dream without regard for anything but the potential of God in you.***

Don't let yourself get caught up in how exactly you will get there. New vision requires new action and new understanding, but just because you don't yet know how to accomplish it doesn't mean you can't learn later. For now, just be willing to open your eyes to see it, believe it and begin moving towards it. The gap between here and there, between present circumstances and the future vision, can seem overwhelming, but that's the point! Step out from your past and start seeing what God sees. Start dreaming big dreams.

## Paint It!

Creating vision is not meant to be a tedious task. However, thinking about the big picture of your life does require both time and courage. You have to slow down from the daily rush and intentionally look to see your life in a different way. If you don't have the guts to think bigger, you won't have the guts to live bigger. Looking ahead is a choice that few people believe they have the time for, but those who understand the true value of vision know they can't live without it.

***If you don't have the guts to think bigger, you won't have the guts to live bigger.***

It can be hard to start thinking bigger, especially if it's been a while since you last tried it. Here are a few things you can do to stimulate your thinking when it feels like a challenge.

1. **Dream with God.** Proverbs 25:2 says that, "It is the glory of God to conceal a matter, but the glory of kings is to search out a matter." Start asking God to expand your thinking, to help you search and to start inspiring you with what He has in mind. He may give you dreams while you sleep or a new idea while you're brushing your teeth. Be open and ready at any moment for God to speak. It can start with a simple prayer of, "God, put your dream in my heart and show me what's possible."

2. **Write your wants.** You aren't alive to live each day waiting for your next set of orders. You have wants and desires for a reason, so don't be afraid to express them. They don't always come easily, but once you start paying attention to them, they begin to flow with greater ease. Write the title for your vision at the top of a page and start listing everything that comes to mind.
3. **Seek council.** Mentorship is a powerful way to enlarge your life. Those who have been where you are, or who are experts in your areas of need, can provide you with both hope and a strategy for success. You can share your problem and use their expertise to see beyond the issue and into the promise of overcoming it.
4. **Learn something new.** If you have trouble finding a mentor in the flesh, all is not lost. One of the easiest forms of mentorship is through reading. You can go to the library and find dozens of books written about how to solve your problem. By learning something new and by studying those who have gone before us, we can think in bigger, better and more effective ways.
5. **Build a vision board.** You can find and keep your inspiration, though challenging, with a vision board. This project involves going through magazines, books and websites looking for pictures that encapsulate the life you are partnering with God to create. It may consist of pictures of the countries you want to visit, the home you want to own, the book you want to write, the body you want to develop or anything else that is part of your dream. The pictures help assemble the complete vision and having

them together fuels your focus and inspiration each day.

## Feel It!

No matter how detailed a vision is, it is only as effective as the emotions that it creates in you. Anyone can write a list of generic wants. But if your vision doesn't stir up passion, then it isn't worth your time and it won't push you all the way to the end.

As you begin to create your vision, remember to test it. In your mind's eye, see your list as though it is already real. Does it feel exciting? Does it pull you or is it just ok? If it doesn't deeply matter to you, then it isn't a good enough vision. Make adjustments as you go and revisit it every day until you can condense it down into a list, a paragraph or even a single statement that truly moves you.

## Target Your Values

To best maximize your inspiration, you need to connect your vision to the things you value most. For example, if you want to improve your physical health, but you value family relationships or career advancement more, then you must organize your thoughts in a way that connects these values to better health. In this case you might identify that being healthy and physically fit will help give you the energy you need for your relationships to flourish and your career aspirations to become a reality. You will have a more balanced mood, making it easier to let offenses go, and a clearer, more creative mind for problem solving in your business.

I know a man who couldn't find the motivation to lose weight for his family, but when he dreams of making a difference in his community, he can't wait to get fit. By connecting your vision to your values, it becomes easier to work at it and therefore, much more likely that you will be successful.

Your vision has the power to truly move you! The key is that you make it fit with your own heart.

## Keep It Positive

To keep your vision positive, focus on what you want, not on what you are trying to eliminate or avoid. Instead of, "I will not lose my home," take a more positive approach like, "I will make enough money to pay my bills, invest in my future, give to those in need and enjoy my daily life."

Focusing on the negative in life can sabotage you. As you now know, what you focus on is where you go and what you become. It might seem logical to make a list that includes, "I won't go bankrupt" or "I won't be overweight." However, you are painting a negative picture for your future and you are keeping your thinking too small.

The solution: stay away from all references to the defeat you are trying to overcome and instead, keep your sights on the victory ahead. Make your vision a positive one, full of what you want to accomplish and not what you want to avoid.

## Get It Done

As you craft your own vision, consider these example statements. Notice that they all have the following qualities in common:

1. **Positive.** To keep you focused on where you're going and what you want to accomplish.
2. **Descriptive.** To make it real to your imagination as you see and experience every last detail.
3. **First person.** So your brain knows it's for you and not for a stranger.

4. **Present tense.** To create a true sense of ownership that activates jeopardy.

These qualities, as well as connecting it to your values, help to generate the emotions you need for real impact. But remember, feelings are subjective, so these statements may not all resonate with you. What's important is that your vision feels great to you.

A vision for your family may include:

- I have a passionate love and devotion for my husband/wife that makes me excited to come home from work every night.
- My family is deeply connected with one another, always seeking to honour God in everything we do.
- My children love each other and respect and honour their parents.
- My home is a place that cultivates the presence of God that brings peace and healing to our visitors.
- My family knows beyond a shadow of a doubt, who they are, why they are here and where they are going.
- Together, we know and operate in our natural and spiritual gifts to a degree that changes the lives of everyone we encounter.

A vision for your body may include:

- I weigh 190 pounds and have 15% body fat.
- My blood pressure reads 120/80.
- I have the physical and mental endurance to run a full marathon.
- I have the ability to play in the yard with my grandchildren and to celebrate life with them with non-stop energy.

- I am an inspiration for others to overcome their own life problems.
- I have a clear mind that is able to focus and create.
- I feel amazing about myself, my life and my body.
- I can wear whatever I want and feel great.

**Up Next**

With a clear vision, you set the stage for a whole new set of stories that support the life you were made to live. Now we can move foward and identify the empowering truth, beginning with identity.

# Chapter 7
# Your New Identity: Becoming Unstoppable

A gap exists for most people between who they really are and how they view themselves. Until you see what God sees and believe what He believes, you will never be able to live the full life He has for you. The closer you get to accepting your true identity, the more freedom and victory you can experience.

I believed for years that I had nothing to contribute to the world. I thought my opinions didn't matter, that I wasn't good enough to offer anything of value, and that if I opened my mouth, I would be ignored or criticized. As a result of my weak identity, I lived in constant fear of being found out, so I stayed quiet and out of the way, despite how desperately I wanted to break free.

I, like so many people today, found myself a prisoner behind the bars of a negative and destructive sense of self. Fear, anxiety and apathy held me, symptoms that showed how I thought too little of myself. But, thank God, those prison bars were never made for me, or for you.

What you believed yesterday or even today doesn't have to hold you down. You no longer need to sit and cope with pain.

You can choose to believe something new and you can allow God to work on your heart and your mind. Together, you can rewire how you think and redefine your self-image. Your true identity is already yours. It's just waiting for you to step out and live it.

***Your true identity is already yours. It's just waiting for you to step out and live it.***

## Identity by Choice

You had no power to choose your beliefs while you were young, but you do have that power now. It's not a matter of trying to remember the hundreds or thousands of events from your childhood that shaped what you believe today. That would drive you crazy. Instead, you have the freedom to make a choice to move forward and start believing something new right now, regardless of the past.

You can identify the truth, choose to believe it and then make room for God to bring healing wherever necessary. Take up your right to step in and become a co-author in writing a new story. You have the authority to decide what you want to believe, and the power to make it real. With the right keys to access your own heart, everything can change.

***You have the authority to decide what to believe, and the power to make it real.***

It all begins with taking responsibility for your current state. Not because it's your fault, but because it's your opportunity to grow and change. A lot of things happen to us without our consent, but as long as we assign blame, we lose our authority to choose. Instead, we remain defined by other people and the circumstances that hurt us.

God has made you able to join Him is writing your true identity into your belief system. The question is, are you willing to believe something new? Are you willing to say no to the fear that tries to hold you back and yes to the potential that's deep inside of you? No belief that you have is truly permanent if you don't want it to be, but you have to make the choice to abandon it.

You are incredible, beautiful, lovable, brilliant, accepted and so much more. You may not believe it yet, but all that I ask is that you open yourself up to be willing to believe something new about yourself. You don't need to have all the answers or the steps figured out. There were years in my life that I worried I wasn't doing the right things for God to be able to "fix" me. What I came to realize, however, was that my intention and desire to change were all that He needed. God knows the problems you face as well as all the steps for transformation. Trust Him in the process because He is both willing and able to heal your heart and reveal your true identity.

## Identity by Potential

*Potential Factor #1: You Are Not Your Labels*

Labels are all the negative ways we define ourselves, such as ugly, stupid, unwanted or lazy. We all struggle with our own list of destructive definitions. As imperfect people, we make mistakes and we judge ourselves by them. In addition, other people call us names in school and we learn to measure ourselves next to cultural standards that are often unrealistic. As a result, we live with a steady focus on our limitations, and by the law of vision, where we focus is where we stay.

Every unhealthy label robs you of your true self. The truth is that all of these limiting beliefs and defeating choices are unworthy of you, because you have a new nature (2 Corinthians 5:17). We have been reborn into the image of God Himself and, let me assure you, God does not make mistakes. This means that every time we falter we are living below our true nature.

***Every time we falter, we are living below our true nature.***

We struggle with addictions, but we are no longer addicts. We have a habit of lying, but we are no longer liars. Regardless of what you do, if it's less than what God would do, then it's not the real you. You may have committed the worst acts you can imagine, but God's promises have nothing to do with severity. You can be forgiven of all and made entirely brand new.

It is essential you understand that you are NOT defined by your choices, past mistakes or the opinions of others. You are defined by the new nature inside of you.

If you label yourself a liar, cheater, smoker, procrastinator or as ugly, stupid or fat, you are allowing God's best to be stolen from you. It's time to remove these unhealthy labels and replace them with truth. God has saved and redeemed you, called you by name and given you a destiny and a purpose. Now you have to believe it.

*Potential Factor #2: You Are Not Your Inner Narrative*

The inner dialogue that runs through our minds all day long isn't our true nature either. Negative thought patterns are exhausting when they keep happening day after day. It starts to feel as though they must reflect who we are and what we believe. Why else would they be there all the time, right?

The truth is that your troubling thoughts are the product of unhealthy beliefs trying to help you (recall ANTs from chapter 2). Just because you have a thought doesn't make it true, nor does it mean you actually believe it. However, once a thought becomes part of your daily thinking, it becomes yours to manage.

Struggling with anger or lust does not make you an angry or lustful person. Your challenge to stay focused doesn't mean you are dumb or hyperactive. That voice inside your head that keeps identifying your flaws isn't right just because it exists. Rather, you must filter and test it to the same degree as the opinions of others. If a complete stranger walked up to you and called you stupid without any provocation, would you believe it? I sure hope not. In the same way, we need to judge the accusations and limitations of our own thinking.

***We need to judge the accusations and limitations of our own thinking.***

The reality is that all kinds of thoughts come and go. When we fail to manage our thought lives, those thoughts can become predominantly negative and destructive. They aren't our nature, they are our habit. Thankfully, the real you is able to hear and judge every word that passes through your mind. Each unwanted thought can be cast down and put away because it isn't you and it isn't true. You are greater than your thought life.

*Potential Factor #3: You Are Not Your Feelings*

Feelings come from many places. Let's look briefly at five of them: belief, focus, environment, circumstance and God. Just like labels and inner narrative, they do not define you.

When an experience touches a **belief**, it produces a feeling. For example, a woman who believes that she is insignificant is likely to feel insecure while in a large group. She may interpret that feeling as evidence that her belief is true and she is indeed insignificant. The truth, however, is that the feeling of insecurity is merely the result of a lie that gets turned on in group settings.

Feelings from **focus** are related to our inner narrative. When we focus on something and give it a negative meaning, we, not surprisingly, generate a negative feeling within ourselves. Can you think of a time when you obsessed over something you didn't want to happen? It might have been dreading an exam, speaking in public or a confrontation with another person. Rehearsing in your mind just how badly it would go created feelings of fear and dread. That experience didn't mean you are a naturally fearful person, but rather that you generated fear through unhealthy focus.

Our physical **environment** also plays a big part in how we feel. Certain colours and smells can make you more alert or more relaxed. The emotions of the people around you can change your own state, causing you to "catch" their moods. This is because your brain looks into the world and attempts to reproduce what it sees. So although an environment triggers a real feeling, it isn't about you.

**Circumstance** is an easy one to understand. We all have good days and bad ones that make us feel a whole range of emotions. You can lose a job, get in a fight, make a huge sale or have your coffee paid for by the car in front of you in the drive-through. None of these things are your nature, yet they all make you feel something.

Sometimes **God** Himself moves your emotions in order for

you to understand what He thinks and wants in a particular situation. It could be a burden to pray for a friend, compassion to buy lunch for a homeless person or unconditional love to forgive someone who hurt you. God does this in you so you can connect with Him and follow His lead. Essentially, if He can impact the way you feel, He can influence your decisions.

As you can see, your feelings have many sources, but none of them should define you. Just because you have been feeling angry lately doesn't make you an angry person. Nor does envy make you ungrateful or sadness make you depressed. Negative feelings exist to alert you to a problem, not to express your identity.

***Negative feelings exist to alert you to a problem, not to express your identity.***

*Potential Factor #4: It's In Your True Nature*

Our thoughts, feelings and actions are meant to flow in only one direction: out from who we are, to express our true selves. Although we all make mistakes, nothing that we think, feel or do can flow back to define us. Our identity is the DNA of our lives.

Your physical DNA lives inside the nucleus of every cell in your body. Just outside of the nucleus is another structure called the Golgi Apparatus. (Don't worry, this didn't just turn into a biology textbook!) Here's the takeaway: the Golgi Apparatus allows things to flow out from your DNA, but it blocks everything on the outside that tries to flow back in. In other words, it's a one-way valve that protects the core of your physical being.

The same principle is true for your nature in Christ. Your spiritual identity can never be tainted or tarnished. Anything less than who you really are is only a false perception and a lie. Just like with your DNA, nothing and no one but God can get in to change the real you. The nature He has given you can never be stolen or erased. It can only be hidden from sight.

In essence, the real you is who you would be if you had no limitations. We often act out of habit or to escape some kind of pain, rather than to do what's best in any given moment. Think of a recent mistake that you wish you could take back. If you did it all over again, what would you do differently? The healthy and productive choice that you're thinking of is your highest self: your true nature.

***The real you is who you would be if you had no limitations.***

So if our true nature would always make the right choice, then what's the problem? Why do we make so many mistakes? The reality is that our past hurts and unhealthy beliefs get in the way and block the expression of our true selves. Your God-ordained identity gives a direction, but like the game of broken telephone, it passes through your heart stories and becomes a completely different message. This means your mistakes and bad habits don't make you a bad person. They simply reveal a faulty story.

The solution? Change the story! Stop identifying with your limitations. Regardless of what has happened around you, in you, through you or to you, you are far greater than it all. You are not your mistakes, weaknesses, sins, actions, roles or fears. You are your Father's son or daughter. You are your spiritual identity, which is in the process of being uncovered.

You are already the person that God has created you to be. Your spirit, unrestricted by the hurts and faulty beliefs of your soul, is your true self. As your heart is healed and you believe the truth, your spiritual identity is revealed to you more and more. It doesn't matter how many mistakes you have made, your identity and your amazing value, just like your DNA, can NEVER be erased.

You have already received a new nature in Christ and your heart and mind simply need to catch up. You have been *reborn* into the image of God and you are being *transformed* into His likeness. You are becoming more like Him in your thoughts, feelings and actions every single day. If you sprained your ankle, would you call yourself disabled? No! You would see yourself as hurt, but in the process of healing towards your true, healthy self. It's worth saying again: you are who you would be if you had no limitations because you have been given a new, perfect nature.

## Identity by Christ

When you accept God's gift of salvation, your old nature passes away and you receive a new identity. When God looks at you now, He sees His Son. All of the love that He feels for Jesus, He feels for you. You are as white as snow and more precious than all the wealth in the world.

The most important thing you can ever know about yourself is that you are a beloved son or daughter of God. As you discover more about what that means, you will begin to experience real and lasting fulfillment and security. While not an exhaustive list, here are a number of truths that you can now choose to believe about yourself.

**You are CHOSEN**

Ephesians 1:4 – "Just as He chose us in Him before the foundation of the world, that we would be holy and blameless before Him."

**You are FORGIVEN**

Psalm 103:12 – "As far as the east is from the west, so far has He removed our transgressions from us."

**You are ADOPTED**

John 1:12 – "Yet to all who received him, to those who believed in his name, he gave the right to become children of God."

**You are LOVED**

Romans 8:38-39 – "For I am convinced that neither death nor life, neither angels or demons, neither the present nor the future, nor any powers, neither height nor depth, nor anything else in all creation, will be able to separate us from the love of God that is in Christ Jesus our Lord."

**You are VALUED**

Matthew 10:30 – "But the very hairs of your head are all numbered."

**You are KNOWN**

Psalm 139:1b – "You have searched me and known me."

**You are HAND-MADE**

Psalm 139:13-16 – "For You formed my inward parts; you wove me in my mother's womb. I will give thanks to You, for I am fearfully and wonderfully made; wonderful are Your works, and my soul knows it very well. My frame was not hidden from You, when I was made in secret, and skillfully wrought in the depths of the earth; Your eyes have seen my unformed substance; and in Your book were all written the days that were ordained for me, when as yet there was not one of them."

**You are CELEBRATED**

Zephaniah 3:17 – "The LORD your God is in your midst, a victorious warrior. He will exult over you with joy, He will be quiet in His love, He will rejoice over you with shouts of joy."

**You are NEVER ALONE**

Deuteronomy 31:6 – "Be strong and courageous, do not be afraid or tremble at them, for the LORD your God is the one who goes with you. He will not fail you or forsake you."

**You are a FRIEND**

John 15:15 – "No longer do I call you slaves, for the slave does not know what his master is doing; but I have called you friends, for all things that I have heard from My Father I have made known to you."

**You are VICTORIOUS**

Philippians 4:13 – "I can do all things through Him who strengthens me."

All of these truths, while difficult to accept at first, will profoundly transform your life as they move from your head to your heart. Learning to believe what God believes about you is the best gift you can give to yourself. It sets you free to be the person who God made you to be—with no limitations.

***Learn to believe what God believes about you.***

## Identity by Vision

To escape the hidden forces that keep you the same, and to become free to change your life, each of your stories must point towards your vision. This picture of the future offers direction in the process of transforming your sense of self. I would never suggest that you build your identity on the things you want. However, you do need your identity to grow in a way that allows those new things to be possible.

***You need your identity to grow in a way that allows new things to be possible.***

If your vision is to be healthy and fit, then you need to decide to see yourself as that kind of person. To become fully devoted and loving towards your spouse, you must view yourself as one who is loving, devoted and perhaps compassionate, forgiving and romantic. You have the capacity to believe whatever is supportive to your vision. You just need to make that choice.

Do you really believe that your vision is possible? If you do, then what does it mean about you? Every limitation that currently exists inside your self-image is a lie, and the more you begin to act in ways that support your vision, the more you will begin to see your true self.

**Up Next**

With your true identity in mind, we will turn our attention to values. It's time to create the inner drive that helps to carry you to victory.

# Chapter 8
# Your New Values: Creating Inner Drive

No one wants to value the wrong things in life, but it happens to the best of us. We don't often make a conscious decision to start living in the opposite direction of our goals, but that happens too. Things change in our value system by tiny little increments, like turning to the right one little degree at a time until we are facing the other way. While it takes time to get to the wrong place, it can feel like it happens overnight.

The gradual shift is a result of our daily decisions. The heart is malleable, so when we take consistent steps outside of our normal choices, our beliefs and feelings readjust to accept and support the new direction. One may choose to work late two nights a week to stay ahead, reduce stress at home and be fully present with family. While a very noble cause, those two nights of overtime can quickly become three, four or five, and then weekends as well.

It begins when you make a small decision that pushes the boundaries of your personal standards. You know it isn't the healthiest choice, but it's easy and you can find a way to justify it in the moment. Unfortunately, when you repeat something enough times, it becomes the new "normal" for you. And once something feels normal, you stop questioning it and your standards shift to include it. It is no longer outside of your comfort zone, but absorbed into it.

As time progresses in a marriage, for example, date nights happens less and less frequently and the relationship becomes a little less connected. One spouse begins to spend a little extra time with a coworker. Innocent joking leads to flirting, which then eventually leads to a full-blown emotional affair. I'm not suggesting that missing date night means you're heading towards an affair, but the reality is that our biggest mistakes start with daily compromises. A healthy and loving relationship doesn't just fall apart in a day. It breaks down through a series of seemingly small incremental steps in the wrong direction.

***Our biggest mistakes start with daily compromises.***

When you are unintentional about what you want your values to be, they are more than happy to sort themselves out by adjusting to the way you think and act most of the time. Your feelings, values and desires follow the lead of your actions and, "suddenly", you want different things. Simply put, where you invest your time and energy is where your values will go. Whatever you justify, no matter how noble or evil it may be, sets in motion a change of heart. No matter how much you want the old life back, you have trained your heart to feel differently.

We are all in a constant state of change because each new experience and choice creates an opportunity to become different. What you feel and believe today won't necessarily be what you feel and believe a year from now. That's great news for all of us. It means that no matter where we are in life, we can grow and change until we reach our destination. If you want your dream to be truly meaningful, you have the power to make that choice.

## Choose the "Right" Values

If we have the power to choose what matters most, both intellectually and emotionally, then we need to identify the right values for our goals. We are compelled to say yes to the things we love and no to the things we don't, so we need to ask: what "yes" will be most supportive? What new standards can we set for ourselves that will guarantee the right results?

As you will recall, our C.O.R.E. values are made up of life *Categories*, *Other* people, our *Roles* and our personal style of *Expression*. You have the power now to choose what will take precedence. There may be things that have taken priority in your life that no longer belong at the top. What should take their place?

If your goal is to lose weight, then you may list health, self-control and physical energy among others. A stronger relationship might require a focus on family, personal connection and adventure. Whatever your goal or vision may be, any change in lifestyle requires a corresponding change in values.

Don't worry if your new list doesn't connect with you yet. The more you choose to live these values, the more natural they will become as your brain accepts them as normal. Your emotions will adapt and begin to support the cause before you know it.

## Feed the Starving Values

In order to consistently make better choices, we need to stop living from a sense of lack. When a personal value goes unfulfilled for too long, it rises to the top of our priority list and acts out in whatever way will bring quick satisfaction. It isn't concerned about your health or its long-term impact, just that the pain goes away.

***In order to consistently make better choices, we need to stop living from a sense of lack.***

When you learn to satisfy your unmet values in healthier ways, you can help prevent the self-sabotaging urges that keep getting in your way. Without the feeling of starvation, those unhealthy behaviours no longer serve a purpose in your life. You are finally able to do the things that move you in the right direction without a yo-yo effect kicking in and sending you back to the starting line.

As you begin to choose new values and to reprioritize your daily life, remember that we all have values that can't be sacrificed or removed. These include universal needs like love, acceptance and security, as well as adventure, solace or meeting new people. No value is inherently bad, so don't start neglecting some in the name of goal achievement. The only way to safely install new top priorities is to continue satisfying your other values in healthy ways.

Here are examples of how to feed your starving values.

| Value | Craving | Well-Fed Choice |
|---|---|---|
| Significance | Controlling, aggressive and refuse to be wrong so others will know that you're "important". | Become a Big Brother or Big Sister and start investing in someone's life. |
| Acceptance | People pleasing so others won't reject you for being different. | Expand your inner circle by joining a social group that revolves around a personal interest, so you can connect with people who understand you. |
| Stability | Overeating, binge drinking or extreme control over self (ex. anorexia) to exert some level of control in the midst of what feels like chaos. | Seek a counselor, mentor or coach who can help you to better organize your life and see your circumstances in a more empowering way. |
| Financial Security | Greed and hording to prevent loss, rather than produce wealth. | Work with a financial planner who can explain how to meet your financial needs with a practical plan of action. |
| Adventure | Serial dating and excessive shopping or partying in an attempt to seek novelty and thrill, because everything else in life feels dull. | Choose five novel things that would excite you—such as an exotic trip, backwoods camping, skydiving or a dance class—and start booking them. |

## Wield Your Values for Good

When we give up on a goal, we often explain it with, "I guess it didn't matter that much to me after all." That's probably true, but it doesn't mean you weren't capable of caring more about it. Most often, it really does matter, but we have failed to connect the dots between vision and values. We can't rely on our feelings and desires to take care of themselves. We have to activate them by choice.

***We can't rely on our feelings and desires to take care of themselves.***

The purpose of identifying your values is to align your emotions with your goals, and to do the things that create lasting fulfillment. Vision, when designed to serve your values, becomes a source of exhilarating inner drive. As you gain access to the needs and desires of your own heart, you have the power to leverage them for your benefit.

In my own story, I finally lost the thirty extra pounds by appealing to my existing value system. I felt empowered to make better choices after getting clear on two things that I already cared about: my ability to help others improve their lives and my need for stability and control. Once I understood these values, I could use them to my benefit.

First, I acknowledged that my credibility as a coach and teacher was being compromised. How could I help others overcome issues that I wasn't willing to fight, and how could they trust my insights? If I was going to be serious about making a difference, I had to live the life I preach—which happens to align nicely with my high desire for integrity and respect. I also got clear on exactly how out of control my life and eating had become. Although I couldn't control every circumstance around me, I could choose to control the quality of foods that went into my body.

After identifying the damage I was doing to my top values, I began connecting these needs to my vision. I saw myself standing on stages around the world in front of thousands of people, helping them live better lives. I was making a difference and maintaining my integrity.

I also envisioned myself in a calm, productive state regardless of my situation. Despite the chaotic nature of life, I was fully engaged and at peace. Connecting to my vision inspired me to make better choices each day and placed a higher demand on me to reprioritize my values.

Lastly, I connected my new choices and habits to the values they needed to serve. In the process of getting my health back on track, I often had to sacrifice convenience in favour of contribution and control. However, as Bob Proctor teaches, "sacrifice is giving up something of a lower nature to bring in something of a higher nature." This is what wielding your values is able to do for you. Although convenience was nice, and I did find ways to incorporate it into my new plan, it was worth sacrificing because there were other things that meant so much more to me.

It can feel horrible at first to sacrifice what you want right now for something that promises to be better. But as you see the impact of bringing your highest values into existence, that initial sense of loss is quickly forgotten. The things that mean the most to you are worth the sacrifice of those below it. Often times, we make consistent choices in favour of our lowest values, simply because we are unaware of the impact it is having on the higher ones.

To summarize, wielding your values happens in three ways. First, you identify exactly how your current choices are compromising what you deeply care about so the pain and tension of injustice can get to work. When you take a serious look at what your choices are REALLY costing you, your old excuses just don't seem to provide the same level of comfort any more.

Second, you attach vision to values. Your big, hairy, audacious and inspiring future can be a source of real strength when it serves your needs. As you imagine exactly how your vision will feed those top values, you create an emotional promise of fulfillment and satisfaction and help to minimize the pain of resisting your "starvation cravings".

Third, you connect your new behaviours and habits to the things you value and allow yourself to experience the pleasure and fulfillment of satisfying those needs. In essence, you convert your values into actions and live each day with intention. Now you can no longer justify poor choices, because your standards are raised and the short-term pleasures of compromise just don't seem as appealing as they once did.

**Up Next**

The framework for your inner world is taking shape. The next step is to reconstruct your view of the outside world, so you can break through the invisible barriers that have held you back until now.

# CHAPTER 9
# YOUR NEW WORLDVIEW: BREAKING INVISIBLE BARRIERS

Your worldview is always at work in your life. This lens through which you view the world influences what you see, the meanings you assign to your experiences and ultimately, how you feel and act from moment to moment. If you feel helpless to change, you may have learned to expect each new situation to have the same old limitations. You are stuck because you have been taught to stop looking for new options.

***If you feel helpless to change, you may have learned to expect each new situation to have the same old limitations.***

Thankfully, your brain can change. You have the power to redefine the people, places, roles and things in life, choosing to see them in a way that empowers you. You can question your beliefs, challenging those that defeat you and replacing them with the truth.

As you eliminate the old and make room for the new, life takes on a whole new dimension. You no longer feel helpless, unfulfilled or frustrated with the same old cycles. It's time to shift your focus, see new things and start to live from a new sense of reality.

## Get Possible, Positive, Harmonized & Empowered

Vision is where you want your life to go, but when a worldview builds a wall, you get stuck. In order to break down the barrier and begin to live and move in the right direction, you need to step into a worldview that is possible, positive, harmonized and empowering.

### *Get POSSIBLE*

It doesn't matter how badly you want a goal. If everything in you expects total failure, you can slip into a state of what psychologist Martin Seligman calls, Learned Helplessness. When this happens, you believe that you have no control or power to create change. Instead of chasing after the desires of your heart, you take a step back and settle for whatever feels safe and certain. A worldview that sees possibility, however, anticipates that hard work will pay off with some level of success.

Jesus said, "All things are possible to him who believes" (Mark 9:23). If we expect failure, we fail. If we expect success, we have a far greater chance. This means that the restrictions and boundaries in life are often self-imposed by our beliefs. We need to stop investing our energy in proving why our dreams will never happen and start shifting our focus towards what makes them possible.

***The restrictions and boundaries in life are often self-imposed by our beliefs.***

Here is how a worldview becomes possible.

| OLD Worldview | NEW Worldview |
|---|---|
| People are born with a specific IQ, so I will always be dumb. | Intelligence is a process of learning, so where I am now is not where I will be in the future. |
| Adults can't change. | The brain is designed to change, so no matter what I am struggling with now, I can and will overcome. |
| Fate determines life events. | Life is cause and effect. |
| Body shape and weight is all about genes. | My body has an ideal size and shape, but it does not include being overweight, so I can play a role in attaining great health. |
| There is never enough time. | Time is limited, but the resources exist to get the job done. |

*Get POSITIVE*

An effective worldview anticipates a positive outcome. If you secretly think that success will cause you more pain than staying the same, you will never offer your full effort. Giving up an addiction or an unhealthy habit often means losing a source of immediate comfort and pleasure. While there are certainly physiological factors to manage in addiction, we have to consider the emotional component as well.

If success is defined as the absence of pleasure, along with the promise of pain, your brain will block your efforts to change. It is critical that you see it through a lens that promises pleasure and fulfillment greater than any pain that might come along.

***If success means the absence of pleasure and the promise of pain, your brain will block your efforts.***

Here are a few examples of more positive worldviews.

| OLD Worldview | NEW Worldview |
|---|---|
| Life without drugs is excruciating. | God is the ultimate source of comfort and peace. |
| Work is where I fail. | Work is an opportunity to learn and grow from every mistake. |
| Going home means another fight. | Home can be how we choose it to be. |
| The kitchen is where I give in to cravings. | The kitchen is where I nourish my body and fuel my goals. |

*Get HARMONIZED*

A harmonized worldview supports the person you really are and the life you want to live. In other words, it fits with your identity and values. You might think that a new set of choices is exactly what you need. However, if your heart, by a faulty worldview, believes those new choices will hurt you, make you into someone you dislike, or steal your joy, then you will avoid or quit before you get very far.

***A harmonized worldview fits with your identity and values.***

You can believe in your ability to generate more wealth, but if you define wealth as something that makes you a bad person (and you don't want to be a bad person), then you won't pursue wealth. If you want to lose weight, but you believe that thin people are abused, then your new meal plan will likely fail. If you are trying to connect better with your wife, but think real men don't show emotion, then you may shut down before things go too deep. All the pieces need to fit together.

Consider these examples of how a disagreement can exist between an identity or value and a worldview.

| Identity | OLD Worldview | NEW Worldview |
|---|---|---|
| I'm the kind of person who helps others succeed. | Money is the root of evil. | Money is a tool to make a difference in the world. |
| I am lovable. | Overweight people are happy and well-liked. | Happiness and healthy relationships are the result of choices, not shapes. |
| I am a real man. | Real men don't show emotion. | Real men are courageous enough to let others see them for who they are and what they feel. |

| Value | OLD Worldview | NEW Worldview |
|---|---|---|
| Generosity and connection | Money makes you selfish and lonely. | Wealth creates opportunities to be generous and connected. |
| Productivity and achievement | Taking breaks will make me less successful. | Regular breaks make me more energized and productive, so I can do more in less time. |

### *Get EMPOWERED*

Lastly, an effective worldview empowers you. It breaks off the chains of limiting beliefs that restrain your life by inspiring you to act and making it safe to be flawed. An empowering worldview supports you in your efforts, encourages you through your trials and picks you back up when you fall. It goes beyond being possible and promises that you have what it takes.

***Empowerment goes beyond possible and promises that you have what it takes.***

When I first stepped into a leadership position, I believed that good leaders have all the answers. At the time, I knew a number of strong leaders who always seemed to know what to do. I know now that my assumption was far from the truth, but at the time, I assumed they had it all together.

My definition of leadership left me feeling gun shy. I didn't want to make a decision unless I was absolutely certain it would work. Needless to say, I rarely made any decisions. I was disempowered by my own definition and was equally empowered once I recognized and changed it. I was finally able to be myself and to do what I thought was best. Mistakes happened, and they still do, but I found out that as long as we are allowed to make them, and learn from them, we advance much further and faster in every area of life.

Here are a few examples of a worldview becoming more empowering.

| OLD Worldview | NEW Worldview |
|---|---|
| A good mother doesn't worry about her own needs. | Good health makes me a better mom. |
| A good leader is never wrong. | Good leaders do the best they can with what they have. |

| OLD Worldview | NEW Worldview |
|---|---|
| Women aren't as successful as men at business. | Women have complementary strengths that improve the workplace and make for effective business people. |
| Success is having everything I want. | Success is loving what I do and helping others in the process. |
| People love me when I succeed. | People love me for me. |
| Only people over 30 are taken seriously. | Age is not a prerequisite to make a difference. |

**Up Next**

The final story is where the rubber meets the road. When you choose to pave the right neural connections, you bring your first three stories, and your vision, to life. Let's move on to your new pathways.

# Chapter 10
# Your New Pathways: Paving the Right Neural Connections

It's time to commit to a new way of life that leads to success. Thank God that we don't have to remain stuck, living in constant aversion from pain or dependence on old pleasures and habits to be happy. Instead, we can choose to take control and commit to manifesting the truth about who we are and what matters most, in the midst of how the world really works. We aren't nearly as powerless as we often believe.

***We aren't nearly as powerless as we often believe.***

Just like your worldview, a large part of changing personal rules is acknowledging them, questioning them and then choosing to live in a new way. Your pathways are physical structures inside your brain that, with the right strategy, can change. The new commitments you establish here will become dominant pathways that direct your life with greater ease.

## Pathway Types

Here is a quick reminder of the pathway types.

*Pathway Type 1: MY PERSONAL PROMISE*

My Personal Promise pathways are expressed by absolute statements and typically begin with the words 'Always' or 'Never'. These are your governing black and white rules. When you act in opposition to them, you feel uncomfortable and even unsafe. In response, you quickly move back into your comfort zone and your familiar self-sabotaging choices.

*Pathway Type 2: MY WAY TO SUCCESS*

My Way to Success pathways are similar to My Personal Promises, but offer more insight into their purpose. They ultimately exist to protect you from what you fear, and to help satisfy your needs and desires. Whether to protect you from inadequacy, rejection and loss, or to experience acceptance and control, your personal guarantees put up a good fight against any threat.

These types of pathways are equations of what action will produce the result you want, and are written as 'If/Then' statements. Even though they may not be rational, they make an emotional promise that is nearly impossible to explain away.

*Pathway Type 3: MY AUTOMATIC ACTION*

My Automatic Action is exactly as it sounds: a prescheduled behaviour that happens without thinking. Triggers include time, location, sound, smell, emotion, another person or a thing in your environment, just to name a few. Your brain believes these actions will protect you from pain, produce a reward or make life easier through habit. When a trigger calls upon the behaviour, you feel what seems to be an irresistible urge. You can resist, but it just makes you feel irritable and anxious.

These pathways are actions expressed as 'When/I Will' statements, because they are scheduled to happen after a trigger. You will find that many flow directly out of the first two pathways. For example, "If I don't speak up, then I can't be wrong" creates, "When in a group setting, I will sit as far away from the main talkers as possible." However, for habitual pathways that have formed from mere repetition, the Automatic Actions may stand on their own.

## Convert Your New Stories

Creating new supportive pathways begins with your true identity, values and worldview. Remember, the purpose of your pathways now is to support your vision. As you convert the new stories, you will find that each one has multiple pathway options. Keep them all targeted in the same direction: towards the end result you want to achieve.

Pathways from NEW Identity:

| I am… | Pathway |
|---|---|
| Smart and able | To always find new and creative ways of doing things. |
| Loved | If I maintain my boundaries, then I will be respected and loved as I deserve. |
| Loving | When I see a good friend, I will smile and offer a hug. |
| Bold and courageous | To always stand up for what is right. |
| Active, vibrant and full of energy | To never give up simply because I don't feel like doing something. |

Pathways from NEW Values:

| I value… | Pathway |
|---|---|
| Achievement | If I take regular breaks, then I will get more done. |
| Acceptance | To always treat myself with respect, so I will be accepted by those who really care. |
| Safety | If I connect with God and develop healthy relationships, then I will feel safe. |
| Love | To never accept less than I deserve in the area of love. |
| Health | When I enter the kitchen, I will drink a glass of water and think about my vision. |

Pathways from NEW Worldview:

| I believe… | Pathway |
|---|---|
| Life is cause and effect. | If I choose my behaviour, then I will feel empowered and in control. |
| Intelligence is a process. | To always do my best. |
| God accepts my weakness. | When I make a mistake, I will forgive myself and move on. |
| Wealth allows for generosity. | If I gain wealth, then I can serve others in bigger ways. |

### Keep Adding to the List

You may look at your new list of pathways and think something is missing. Add a few more from each category that, if you truly believed them, they would make a difference in how you live your daily life.

My Personal Promise:

- To always reframe problems as opportunities.
- To always identify what is within my control.
- To never let past experience shape my current assumptions.
- To always satisfy my needs in healthy ways.

My Way to Success:

- If I keep trying new things, then I will find a way to victory.
- If I speak up, then I will make a difference.
- If I look for a solution, then I will find a way out of trouble.
- If I respect myself, then others will respect me, too.

My Automatic Actions:

- When my savings reaches $1,000, I will invest $950 and treat myself with $50.
- When 4pm comes, I will stretch and go for a walk.
- When I feel inadequate, I will confide in a close friend.
- When I get home from work, I will help with dinner.

Don't expect all of your new pathways to come together in an instant. It takes time to identify the right ones and is perfectly fine for you to start small and let them build as you.

**Up Next**

The new stories you have uncovered so far have the power to change your life. The catch is that they can only work to the degree that you believe them. In the final part of Free to Change, you will learn a practical four-step approach to changing your belief system (and your life) for good.

# PART 3
# PUBLISH YOUR STORIES

# Chapter 11
# Step 1 - Feel the Pain: Getting Unstuck & Hungry for Change

Pain is something that most of us want to avoid as often as possible. Whether it's physical, mental or emotional, we do our best to prevent or minimize it whenever we can. While it may be a logical thing to do, our pain avoidance is so automatic and often unseen, that it becomes a large, but secret, reason for our lack of success.

The reality is that pain can be a very positive contributor to our lives. We get too comfortable at times and need a small dose to alert us to a problem and bring us back to our senses. From the pain of touching a hot stove to the twinge of our guilty conscience, we need to use discomfort for what it is: a tool to create lasting change.

***We need to use discomfort for what it is: a tool to create lasting change.***

## Pain Forces Change

How many stories have you heard of men and women turning their lives around after hitting rock bottom? They may have lost their health, job, money, family or all of the above. It can often seem like a sudden loss, but their demise didn't happen overnight. Countless warning signs lined their road to rock bottom, but change wasn't worth it until disaster struck and there was no other option.

Our lives are largely habitual, especially when things seem to be going well. With all of life's stresses, we don't want the added work of changing something that feels good or at least doesn't seem broken.

Spending more money than you make or eating junk food every day, for example, will eventually lead to problems. However, these habits bring pleasure and their consequences seem so far into the distant future that the effort to change right now just doesn't seem worth it. Plus, because your future self feels like a stranger to your brain,[1] you place far more importance on doing what feels right in the present moment and heavily discount the value of what you stand to gain later.

The problem gets worse. If asked how much you're going to exercise next month, you may say three or four times a week, even though you haven't been to the gym in six months. Why? We look ahead and assume that the challenges facing us today won't be there tomorrow, or that we'll be more motivated to face and overcome them at a later date.

With that expectation, we tell ourselves that the negative behaviour is "just one last time" because we'll do better tomorrow or next week. "I'll just have this one last cigarette" or, "after this piece of cake it's only healthy foods for me!" But as you know, these apparent "last times" are rarely ever the end.

It's clear that your brain may be getting in your way. Not only does it hate to give up today's pleasure to solve tomorrow's problem, it also tricks you into thinking the problem will somehow disappear on its own. In these moments a little pain is exactly what the doctor ordered. It wakes you up and forces you to make a change right now. Not for the sake of future glory some day, but for the relief of your present self.

## Pain Takes Us Out of Faulty Stories

The biblical story of Jericho paints the perfect picture of pain as a means of escape from the prison of faulty beliefs. Before taking the city, Joshua sent in two men as spies to survey the land and its inhabitants. The king of Jericho learned of the spies and sent his own men to capture them.

The king's soldiers chased after the intruders, but failed to find them because a woman named Rahab hid them away. Later that night, once the coast was clear, the two spies were let "down by a rope through the window," on the outside of the city wall (Joshua 2:15). Interestingly, the original Hebrew word used for rope is *chebel*, which also means pain.

The city walls of Jericho had trapped the men, just like an unhealthy belief system does to us. Except in our case, we don't even know that it's happening. Our beliefs feel so natural that we rarely have occasion to notice they exist, let alone to question them. We simply live within their walls, held captive by their rules.

Do you know all of your assumptions about the world? Can you perfectly distinguish the differences between your perceptions and those of your friends, family members or co-workers? Are you conscious of every thought you have and why you think it? The answer to these questions, unfortunately, is no.

***Our beliefs feel so natural that we rarely notice that they even exist, let alone question them.***

Your stories are like a pair of glasses. They create a sense of focus, but you no longer see or feel them once they're on. Your brain filters out the cause of your perceptions and just accepts the information as reality. As a result, we all live in our own personal walled city of Jericho, and until we awaken to the existence of our beliefs, all we are able to do is look through them and live as though they are true.

Pain is what wakes us up and provides an opportunity to step outside of our stories, so that we can view them more objectively. It is not until we are looking at a belief, instead of through it, that we can make a meaningful change. It is only then that we can actively question and replace it with the empowering truth.

***It is not until we are looking at a belief, instead of through it, that we can make a meaningful change.***

## Fighting Pain With Pain

Embracing pain is a surefire way to identify problem stories, but we still need to take action. We must fight past the resistance of giving up something that feels good, or at the very least, something that feels familiar. It could be junk food, procrastination, gossiping or addiction. Whatever your feel-good thing is, it satisfies a desire and, at times, fills a hole. It may provide a false sense of control, safety, power or a simple chemical or sugar rush, all in an attempt to create pleasure, numb pain or a combination of both.

These choice behaviours are tough habits to break. They promise to make us feel good right now and they threaten to leave us in misery if we ever give them up. The problem with a goal is that it requires the pursuit of a potential pleasure (that only your future self can fully enjoy), combined with the loss of what you currently know is "good". This creates tension that fights against change, convincing you to choose comfort and protection over possibility and growth.

If the pain of change feels greater than the pain of staying the same, then change is unlikely to happen. We can know that our addiction is killing us, but if quitting means facing intense emotional hurt, then it becomes much more challenging to quit. How can we expect to change what we're doing if our success will result in hurt?

While vision is a wonderful tool, we can't always begin the battle against pain with the promise of pleasure. At times that pleasure seems too far in the future and the pain all too real right now. In these scenarios, motivation and positive self-talk can't push us through. We need to fight pain with pain by making it hurt more to stay the same than it does to do things differently.

***Make it hurt more to stay the same than it does to do things differently.***

## Now Feel the Pain

If you're tired of feeling stuck in old stories, then it's time to approach change in a new way. Try these methods for leveraging positive pain.

### *Method #1: Pain Through Realism*

Optimism is an important skill in overcoming challenges, but we have to be careful not to look through rose-coloured glasses all the time. We must choose to be painfully honest about our current situation. As long as we ignore our present problems, we will never feel motivated to address the issues that cause them.

***As long as we ignore our problems, we will never feel motivated to address what causes them.***

Jack Welsh is the past CEO of General Electric and a leadership expert. He summed it up well when he said, "You have to see the world as it is, not as you wished it were." Some of us, myself included, have a bad habit of looking on the bright side and thinking that things are better than they realy are. While it's great to stay positive and forward-focused, when we don't allow ourselves to see the problem clearly, we can't take the right steps towards positive change.

Our lack of realism becomes even more of a problem when we slip from optimism into self-deception. Milton Cudney explains in his book, *Self-Defeating Behaviors*, that we often practice two forms of pain-avoidance: minimizing and disowning.

Minimizing is the practice of reducing the severity of our problems. We can do this in a number of ways. For one, we compare ourselves to others with statements like, "I'm not nearly as overweight as my neighbour," or, "I don't drink half as much as my brother does." We can also minimize by convincing ourselves that, "it's really not THAT bad," and, "I can quit any time I want."

This pain-reduction strategy is all about making the problem appear smaller than it really is. Every time we do it, we suddenly don't feel so bad about continuing along the same path towards what we know is an unpleasant end. It eases the conscience and makes us feel better about doing the wrong things.

Disowning is just as it sounds: blaming our problems on other people or circumstances outside of our control. Where minimizing eliminates the need to change, disowning says that we can't even if we try.

We feel justified to stay the same, even though it hurts us, because we didn't cause the problem in the first place. It's the fault of our parents who didn't love us, the world system that won't employ us, the church leaders who don't support us, the boss who won't promote us or the genes that keep us overweight. All of these are ways in which we disown our problems. So instead of taking action towards a new end, we wallow, lick our wounds and keep the self-sabotaging behaviours as a badge of honour that shows the world just how badly we have it.

Cudney explains that minimizing and disowning are both used to reduce the amount of mental and emotional pressure that we feel as a result of our poor choices. As long as we can keep ourselves from feeling bad, there's no real need to change.

***As long as we can keep ourselves from feeling bad, there's no real need to change.***

Pain has the ability to set us free, but we first have to eliminate the excuses. If you need a shot in the arm to start moving, then get uncomfortable and come face-to-face with your current reality. Don't wait until you hit rock bottom where the pain becomes intense and unavoidable. Instead, create an urgency to change now with a clear and honest picture of your current situation.

*Method #2: Pain Through Projection*

Positive vision is a critical tool for both strategy and motivation, but there is a down side. Research shows that vividly imagining a positive future has the potential to create a sense of "Projected Glory".[2] This brain trick makes us feel as though we have already accomplished our goals and that it's time to celebrate. Even though, of course, no ground has been taken yet. We feel satisfied and entitled to take a break or to act against our goals, thinking that we deserve it (recall Moral Licensing from chapter 3).

While it's important to keep an eye towards your amazing future, you also need one looking in the opposite direction of where you're going if you never change. To do so, you must consider where you will be in five, ten or twenty years if you keep doing what you're currently doing.

Will you be overweight, alone, totally broke or even dead? What about your vision and values? Can you feel the disappointment of never attaining your dreams? Can you feel the discomfort of compromising the things you deeply care about?

Projection allows you to visit different versions of your future, so you can stay on the right track every step of the way. You can bring yourself into that potential life and experience the pain of disease in your body, the sorrow of a broken relationship or the frustration of having no money, all within the safety of your imagination. The ability to regret wasted years before they happen is something that can help you make the right choices when you're too comfortable to start or too tired to carry on.

### *Method #3: Respond to Pain as It Happens*

Life is full of discomforts. You can feel on edge around a certain person, angered by the wording of an email, insecure in the midst of "powerful" people or awkward when someone cries. These shifts in state happen all the time, but we often ignore them and then miss out on great opportunities for change.

Each time you feel on edge, angry, insecure, awkward, disgusted, judgemental or afraid is a chance to grab onto the rope called pain and escape from your own walled city of Jericho. In these moments, you can ask, "What story am I telling myself?"

I was out driving one night with a good friend. He knew I was going through a difficult life season and wanted to offer his support. As I expressed just how frustrated I was feeling, he asked me, "But why do you feel that way?" Immediately, a response popped into my mind that I had never thought before: "I'm tired of always being God's second choice."

I had no idea that story existed inside of me until I embraced the pain and took the opportunity to look. I'm certain you have had similar moments or seasons of pain—some big and others small. What matters most is that you don't avoid them. They are trying their best to lead you safely out the window to your freedom.

## But Don't Forget to Forgive

While pain is a great teacher and motivator, it can also be a destructive force that prevents change. When we carry hurts and offenses from the past, we lock ourselves up inside of an emotional prison, waiting for payment from someone who has likely forgotten about the situation. Until we forgive, we remain stuck in the past and unable to ever really heal and move on.

Difficult circumstances and painful experiences create unhealthy life stories that secretly sabotage us and desperately need to be changed. Although a hurt may not be our fault, we must be careful not to assign blame for the way we feel or for what we now believe. When we do this we give the lies permission to remain. This happens for two reasons.

First, every hurt carries a message. The absence of a father's love, for instance, can tell a story of inadequacy and insignificance.

The embarrassment of forgetting your lines in a play or speech may have planted a seed of fear of failure. The loss of a business or relationship might have convinced you that you just aren't good at life. Whatever your own experience was, if a memory still produces a negative feeling then it carries a negative meaning. And as long as you can look back and find proof for your beliefs, you will keep them close to your heart.

***As long as you can look back and find proof for your beliefs, you will keep them close to your heart.***

Secondly, how can we possibly take charge of our own lives and create any kind of improvement if, deep down, we believe that it's not within our power? If uncontrollable forces, like bad circumstances or other people, have created our problems, then we are helpless to change them, right? So we never really try.

As long as we wait for someone else to fix the problem, pay the debt and take away the pain, we are powerless to step into a better life. As victims, we will never become the victors we are meant to be.

The past cannot be undone, but it *can* be retold. Thank God that our memories no longer need to dictate our lives. We can look back and give it all new meaning. We have been given a key to heal from our hurts, replace lies with the empowering truth and escape from the prison of repeating the past. That key is forgiveness.

**Up Next**

Pain initiates the process, but you can't stop there. Unlesss you have hope, you run the risk of getting stuck in the past, where you rebuild the same old walls of self-defeat.

# Chapter 12
# Step 2 - Embrace Hope: The Key to Pushing Forward

Pain is an important part of our change process, acting as a red flag and a catalyst to get us moving. However, it becomes a destructive and demotivating force over the long-term when left on its own. To continue the forward momentum, we need to pair our discomfort with a positive and uplifting reason to advance. In short, pain wakes us up and gets us out of the old story, but it is hope that pulls us into the new one.

## What is Hope?

Before we look at what hope can do for you, let's start with a basic definition. The Merriam-Webster dictionary defines hope as, "to desire with expectation of obtainment." It's wonderful to have a goal or vision you desperately want, but that alone is not enough. You must combine your desire with faith that it will really happen. Hope only comes with a positive expectation of better days ahead. Not simply from desire.

***Hope only comes with a positive expectation of better days ahead. Not simply from desire.***

## Hope as the Exit

Let's look again at the story of Jericho. Before the Israeli spies were let down from Rahab's window, she made them make a promise. She wanted protection for her family on the day of invasion, in return for her good deed. The men agreed, but gave Rahab a condition. She had to hang a red cord from the window so they would know which household was hers.

The rope used for the spies to escape from the city was pain (*chebel*), while the original word used for the cord that saved Rahab and her family is *tiqvah*, which also means hope. On the day the city fell, they were safely extracted from the rubble and joined the Israelites for the rest of their lives.

Here is the three-step process we learn from this illustration. First, pain takes you out of an old story so you can examine it. It helps you recognize that a problem exists, and then question the reality you would otherwise assume to be true. Our stories are invisible, so unless we have a good reason to look, we blindly live within their walls.

Second, truth judges the lie and strategy tears down the old restrictive walls. In the case of Jericho, the Israelites followed God's specific instruction until the city fell. It was His word (truth) and His plan (strategy) that produced the result they wanted.

Finally, hope pulls you from the rubble that could otherwise tie you to the past. It gives you reason to endure the struggle and fight for better days ahead. It becomes your second wind that reinvigorates you and keeps you moving forward.

***Pain takes you out of the old story so truth can tear it down. Then hope pulls you out from the rubble so you can finally move forward.***

Hard times create an opportunity to break down the old beliefs that prevent us from seeing, thinking and living bigger. We can destroy the old invisible limitations if we choose to take that first step out from the city of our faulty beliefs, but it takes guts. If in the midst of the battle of embracing pain and seeking truth, you can look up and out into a future full of hope, you can exit the old and enter the new. It is this last step that we often forget.

Many people go through a crisis in their health or a relationship, for example, and commit to making a change, but then never follow through. Instead, they spend months, or even years, dwelling on the past and wishing things had turned out differently. They felt cheated and deflated, and without a positive expectation for the future, they stayed back for history to repeat itself. In other words, they fell into their same old habits and eventually rebuilt the same old stories and pathways.

This is because breaking habits feels bad. Without hope telling us that stepping out from our comfort zone is worth it, new choices feel like way too much work. As a result, we give up and surrender to the circumstance, blame others for our problems and assume there is nothing we can do about it. With this defeated mindset, we then resume with our old behaviours, which inevitably reinforce our old broken stories. Instead, we must choose to refocus our eyes and strengthen our grasp on hope.

Letting hope in is hard when we feel uncertain about ourselves and beat up by life. We struggle to believe in something better because it carries risk. However, when we work at maintaining our hope, we have a reason to change our minds. It provides a little bit of light, so we can look up from our problems and start walking towards the solution.

In short, when we lose hope, we get stuck. We get held back in cycles of self-fulfilling prophecy, where hard times become more evidence of everything that's wrong with us. Instead of moving out from our defeating stories we merely rebuild the walls by returning to our old habitual way of thinking and living. If we want to safely exit and advance our lives for good, we desperately need hope.

### The Elements of Hope

Dr. Shane Lopez is one of the world's leading researchers on hope. In his book, *Making Hope Happen,* he explains the science behind this powerful force in our lives. In fact, according to Lopez, there are three primary elements that increase the amount of hope we experience on a daily basis.

*Hope Element #1: "The future will be better than the present."*

This is an easy one to understand, and it's something that we have already covered with vision. The more you believe in a positive future that is bigger and better than your current circumstances, the better you feel. Plus, when you genuinely expect great things, your stories naturally begin to adapt in ways that make them possible.

*Hope Element #2: "I have the power to make it so."*

This element of hope is an important piece of an empowering identity and worldview. It is critical that you recognize your own measure of control and influence in the outcome of your life. The law of cause and effect says that what you do matters, and that if you do the right things consistently, then you can reach your envisioned future—at least to some degree.

It's easy to slip into a state of helplessness where we don't think that we can do anything to make a difference. We become apathetic and heartsick as we lose sight of the truth. We need to believe that we are co-authors in life, not just passengers waiting for someone else, including God, to do something.

***We are co-authors in life, not just passengers waiting for someone else to do something.***

*Hope Element #3: "There are many paths to my goals."*

Big vision is really good at compelling you to get up and go, but in order for it to produce a long-term sense of hope, you must convert it into a plan. This is for two reasons. First, vision can seem so great that it overwhelms you. It's exciting at first, but over time it can begin to seem too good and too big for you to ever achieve. Second, vision can seem so far into the future that you begin to question your commitment and how much you really want it.

It's important that you create vision without the concern of planning, because trying to see the path will often keep your thinking too small. However, once it has been crafted, you need a tangible plan that anticipates the challenges and brings the vision to life.

Multiple paths are necessary because unexpected problems happen. When you hit a roadblock on Plan A, you need to be prepared with an alternate route or you start to question the possibility of success and your hope begins to waver. The plan, with its multiple paths, is what takes you from fantasy to a tangible hope that changes you from the inside out.

## Now Go Make Hope

If you want to increase your sense of hope and attach those positive feelings to your new stories, here are a few methods to consider.

*Method #1: Connect Your Vision to the New Stories*

If you haven't created a vision, it's a great place to start. Seeing and expecting a future that's better than your current circumstance is the first element of hope. Once you have vision, or at least a starting point, it's time to connect it to the new stories you want to believe.

Your heart wants to see your hopes fulfilled. As you develop a positive expectation and excitement of brighter days ahead, your stories begin to change. If you truly believe that your vision is possible, there is no more reason to accept the stories that would prevent it. For example, your current self-image may say, "I am poor", but as you begin to believe that your future holds more wealth, your story begins shifting and changing to align with what you see on the inside.

Try this exercise to connect your vision to your new stories.

Step 1: Review your vision and experience it internally with your five senses. Make it real to yourself and feel your emotions lift as hope enters in.

Step 2: In that state of hope, look at your new stories and consider how each one will help lead you to your vision. Don't try to convince yourself of its truth. Instead, focus on its ability to help you get what you want.

Step 3: Journal your progress. There is something uniquely powerful about writing things down. Add strength to this exercise by putting pen to paper and fully exploring each new story and its contribution to your vision.

*Method #2: Make a Tangible Plan*

Big vision takes time to accomplish. There is often a delay between our new choices and the final outcome—sometimes even years. When our desires are drawn out or under long delays, our hope can begin to run dry. We become frustrated and heartsick. When that happens, we slip back into our old ways as we give up on the dream and lose sight of what really matters.

You don't get braces and assume that your teeth will be straight in a week. They come with a clear path and set of expectations that you accept and don't think to challenge. Unfortunately, few things in life are like braces. Despite thinking that we know and believe change takes time, we often secretly expect our relationships to be healed or our bodies to lose weight on day one of the new program.

When we don't see the path or make a plan for each step, we lose perspective and get disappointed too quickly. When hard times come and fear sneaks in, we need confident assurance that it's still worth the fight. We need to know that we're not wasting our time and effort.

So how do you make a great plan? According to Dr. Lopez it needs to have several things.

Step 1: Part A – Start with the best possible plan. What are five things you can do each day to move towards your vision? What five things can you do each week and month? Create your ideal schedule and see the path begin to take shape in front of you.

Step 2: Part B & C – Multiple plans might seem like overkill, but what happens when something unexpected comes your way? If you hit a wall or take a sudden turn, and your plan no longer works, then you're at risk of losing hope. You need backups.

Step 3: Plan for Problems – Nothing can take the wind out of your sail faster than an unforeseen problem. Whether it's the temptation of free donuts at work or the overwhelming stress of hosting a family function, it's important to know your weak spots. When you know what's coming, you can plan accordingly and push past the resistance that would otherwise hold you back.

*Method #3: Put Your Hope in God*

Preparation and planning can only take us part of the way. We must take responsibility for our lives and do all that is within our power, but we also need to rely on God. Times come when problems appear that block our vision of the future and make us feel uncertain, lost and afraid. It is these moments in which hope is most at risk.

We can protect ourselves by putting our hope in God. Isaiah wrote, "Yet those who wait for the LORD will gain new strength;

they will mount up with wings like eagles, They will run and not get tired, They will walk and not become weary." (Isaiah 40:31, NIV).

The original word that Isaiah used for wait also means to look eagerly for, linger for, and expect. When we intentionally look to God for a clearer vision of the future, His support to create change in our lives and a path to get us there, we can expect our strength to be continually renewed. He is not in the business of stealing dreams or breaking hearts. When you have God's promise and you seek Him daily, you can trust in His plans for you completely.

It's important that we don't try to change our lives all on our own, nor that we sit and wait for God to do it for us. Both of these extremes will cause unnecessary delays and a loss of hope. Instead, we need to stay in the balance of doing all we can while maintaining an expectation and dependence upon God. As we live towards the vision with all that we have, our hope and trust in Him will sustain us through the hard times, and carry us through to the end.

*Method #4: Find Success Stories*

Everyone needs encouragement. When life gets tough, our inspiration and hope can suffer. Thankfully, we are not alone. Others have overcome the same challenges we face and their stories can help to relight our fire. Their victories help satisfy the second and third elements of hope, proving that we can make a difference in our own lives and that a path to our success, as impossible as it seems, really does exist.

Watch a documentary, speak to a mentor or read a book written by someone you admire. Any example of personal victory can inspire you during the low times. The key is to hold successful people, and their stories, in your line of sight.

**Up Next**

Pain and hope do more than simply motivate you. They keep you open to seeing and believing something new. Now it's time to focus on letting in the truth. In the next step you will continue your forward momentum with three outer forces that shape your inner world by authoring and activating the right stories.

# CHAPTER 13
# STEP 3 - LOOK UP, OUT & AROUND: USING OUTER FORCES FOR INNER TRIUMPH

The first two steps in this change process are inwardly focused. Now it's time to look at the power of outside forces and how they shape and transform our stories as well. Although we love to think we have total control over our own beliefs and choices, we're not so independent.

Whoever and whatever get our attention most become secret authors of our beliefs and desires. As much as you may try to ignore these influencers, or claim your authority over them, they will eventually break through your walls and change you for better or worse. However, if you learn to take a full inventory of what is up, out and around, you can use these forces to support and ignite your transformation.

***Whoever and whatever get our attention most become secret authors of our beliefs and desires.***

## LOOKING UP

A relationship with God is one of the most powerful ways to transform our inner stories and our lives. As we draw closer to

Him, we change. Does it sound too good to be true? It's not, for a few reasons.

### We Discover Our True Value

Sons and daughters need to know their Father. As created beings, we will never be able to fully appreciate the value inside of us until we know how great and wonderful our Creator is. In essence, we have to know God if we want to truly know ourselves.

***We have to know God if we want to truly know ourselves.***

The biblical story of the prodigal son reveals the importance of knowing the unconditional nature of God's love. In Luke 15, we learn of a son who decides to ask his father for his inheritance early. The father agrees and gives him a share of the wealth. With the cold hard cash in hand, the young man sets off for another country where he lives lavishly and foolishly wastes it all. Just as the son's money runs out, a famine hits the country and he is forced to hire himself out, where he lives and eats with pigs.

One day while lying with the pigs, he has an epiphany. He remembers that even his father's servants are much better off than him. With this in mind, the young man decides to go home, apologize to his father and ask to be made a servant. Because he doesn't know the truth about his dad and the extent of his father's love for him, the prodigal son labels himself as a "worker" in order to feel comfortable enough to go home.

He assumes that his dad would never accept him as his son again after what he has done. However, as soon as he arrives home, he learns the truth. He discovers that his father has been dreaming of his return, ready and waiting to meet him where he is, to embrace him as his son and to welcome him home again.

Here is the lesson. A strong self-image requires a healthy view of God. If you see Him as a harsh judge who is uncaring and distant, you can feel alone and unwanted, and live each day trying to earn your worth. However, when you see Him as loving, compassionate and strong, your sabotaging stories of inadequacy, isolation and weakness fall apart.

***A strong self-image requires a healthy view of God.***

In a similar way, there is a trait of God that repairs each weak link in your identity chain. Whether you struggle with feelings of hate, lust, pride or stupidity, the knowledge of God can help you. Knowing the truth of who He really is breaks off the lies and uncovers your true self.

## We Believe His Word

People in positions of authority secretly (and not so secretly) shape our beliefs. We view them as experts, so we lower the value of our own opinions and elevate theirs in comparison. Even if it conflicts with what we currently believe, we often just accept what a true authority has to say.

In the same way, God can help to alter the stories that won't seem to change. Some lies are so compelling and rooted in fear and pain that our brains fight every attempt to accept the truth. In these cases, we need a trusted Father to enter the scene and help us to believe.

Jesus said, "whoever does not receive the kingdom of God like a child will not enter it at all" (Mark 10:15). We need childlike faith. Think of how you looked up to your parents or guardians when you were young. You thought they were superhuman and had the answers to every question you could think to ask. Because they were so great in your eyes, you believed whatever they said.

Even as adults we lower our guards and become childlike in faith around those who we perceive to be experts in their field. Whether it's a doctor, teacher, leader or industry guru, the higher we position them in our minds, the more likely we are to take them at their word without question.

We need to see God in a similar way. As we elevate our opinion of Him, we begin to approach Him more like a child, willing to believe what He says. Our walls come down and we start to question the things that conflict with His word, simply because He has become a true authority figure in our lives. As we get to know God more, we allow our stories to be rewritten by His truth.

***As we elevate our opinion of God, we become more willing to believe what He says.***

## Wounds Are Healed & Needs Are Met

God wants you to be whole and healthy in your entire being. "He heals the brokenhearted and binds up their wounds," (Psalm 147:3) and He is constantly working towards that end in each of our lives. Sometimes we need to be active participants in the healing process, seeking help from others or working through specific challenges. Other times we experience effortless, and sometimes even spontaneous, change just by spending time with Him in prayer or by reading a portion of scripture that seems to cut to the core of our problem.

David wrote, "You have turned my mourning into dancing;

You have loosed my sackcloth and girded me with gladness, that my soul may sing praise to You and not be silent. O LORD my God, I give thanks to You forever" (Psalm 30:11-12). If God did that for David then He will do it for you too! He takes the most wounded and broken parts of us and allows us to exchange them for wholeness and healing. It's amazing how getting to know the truth about God can mend our wounds.

God also satisfies us emotionally. We are all born with needs, but many of us live our lives without having them fully met. As you have already learned in the Values chapters, unmet needs lead to unhealthy ways of satisfying them. These poor choices set us up for self-sabotage and more hurt. However, when God becomes a source of identity, love, safety, friendship and acceptance, some of our most basic needs are met.

## Now Look Up

You were made to know God and to experience a vast number of benefits from knowing Him. This relationship will change you inwardly so that you can live your true potential outwardly. Consider these ways to start experiencing the results of looking up.

*Method #1: Schedule your daily devotions.*

There is no magical amount of time that you must spend with God every day in order to change. Start by choosing to make Him a priority and connecting with Him at the same time every day. He rewards those who diligently and consistently seek Him (Hebrews 11:6), so make it part of your regular routine.

*Method #2: Determine to know God as Father, Son and Holy Spirit.*
God expresses Himself in three unique persons, and each one has unique attributes. If any one or more of the three seem unclear, distant, unapproachable, uncaring or impersonal, then you are lacking a healthy understanding of God. Try meeting with someone who can teach you, finding a good book or setting out on your own study of scripture.

*Method #3: Stay aware of Him.*
Make it a habit to think about and notice Him throughout the day. Direct your focus upward as often as possible, so that your consistent focus will wire Him into your sense of reality. As He becomes more real to you, healing and change takes place at a deeper level.

## LOOKING OUT

People play an important, and often invisible, role in shaping the stories we adopt and the choices we make. They include our family, friends, teachers, coworkers, bosses and church groups, just to name a few. When we live unaware of their influence, we set ourselves up to fail. Solomon summarized it well when we wrote, "He who walks with wise men will be wise, but the companion of fools will suffer harm" (Proverbs 13:20).

### They Act As Our Mirror

Social Comparison Theory, first proposed by psychologist Leon Festlinger, tells us that we learn about our own beliefs, attitudes and abilities by comparing ourselves to others. As we grow up and try to figure out who we are, what to value, how the world works and how to live, we look at what others do and seem to believe, and then adopt what we observe for our own lives. We assume that if it matters to those closest to us, then it must be important for us, too.

This is especially true whenever we feel insecure, uncertain, inferior, in the midst of crisis, or we just don't have a way to evaluate ourselves. In these moments, we look outwardly to other people for the keys to succeed.

Consider any one of the many stories of high school kids falling into the "wrong crowd" and making a series of unfortunate choices as a result. Adolescence for many is a time of immense change and insecurity. As we seek to understand ourselves and find our place in the world, we often feel stressed out and off-balance. In pursuit of stability, our brains are quick to take on new beliefs and behaviours so that we can be quickly and safely assimilated into a new group.

The effect of our peers, however, goes well beyond just times of uncertainty and stress. According to Lee Ross and Richard Nisbett, two professors of psychology and authors of *The Person and The Situation*, "our most basic perceptions and judgments about the world are socially conditioned and dictated." We are wired to see what others see, believe what others believe and do what others do. Regardless of our life stage, the people we choose to surround ourselves with will help shape how we define both ourselves and the world around us.

***We are wired to see what others see, believe what others believe and do what others do.***

## They Prime Us To Be Like Them

In Bruce Hood's book, *The Self Illusion: How the Social Brain Creates*

*Identity*, he provides countless insights and illustrations of how our beliefs are shaped, often subconsciously, by other people. The Chameleon Effect is one such factor.

You have likely seen or heard of lizards that change their colour to fit safely within their environment. Similarly, we make automatic changes within ourselves in order to fit with our peers. These changes can be as simple as shifting our posture or as extreme as mimicking behaviour or completely altering our mood. Most of the time, though, these alterations happen without our awareness.

Part of their secret power comes from your brain's ability to feel what others feel.[1] When you see someone smile, you want to smile. When you see someone scared in a movie, you feel scared, too. Anxious friends can make you anxious, depressed company can bring you down and an angry mob can awaken the criminal in you. It's not that you are innately wired to be like them, but rather that you have identified with them and your brain is involuntarily feeling what they feel. In those moments you take on a new story and its behaviours as if other people handed them to you.

With this knowledge, you can find ways to prime yourself in the right direction. There are people who will naturally build you up and empower you towards your goals. By witnessing their personality and approach to life, you catch hold of their self-belief and confidence. On the other hand, there are those who drain you and leave you feeling defeated, even without saying much. It's up to you to choose what your brain will reproduce by carefully selecting your closest companions.

***Choose what your brain will reproduce by carefully selecting your closest companions.***

## They Call Us Up or Pull Us Down

The people in our lives have a way of calling us up or pulling us down. Their words, actions and attitudes rub off on us over time, causing us to become more and more like them. As humans, we have a strong desire to belong, and belonging means adopting a common set of beliefs and behaviours.

Whenever you try to make a break from the "group norm", there is friction. Members of the group, whether friends or family, can feel the growing distance between your standards and theirs, and they subconsciously attempt to close that gap by holding you back. It might be jokes about you "eating like a rabbit" when you choose salad instead of the usual pizza. It may be comments about your clothing when you decide to save money and not buy into the newest fashion trend. They don't do it to hurt you. They do it to protect the group as well as themselves.

There is a big part of them that genuinely loves you and doesn't want to lose you. Deep down, they know that if your inner stories and personal standards change, then you will have no choice but to find a new group of friends. Plus, if you have reason to change, and they are a lot like you, then there must be something wrong with them too, right? It's not a nice feeling, so in order to preserve their own self-images, they need to keep you the same.

In addition to fitting in with the group norm, we feel a pull to rise and fall to the expectations of others. When a teacher expects higher grades from us, we perform better.[2] When a manager thinks highly of his or her employee, that employee produces better work.[3] When friends think we're funny, the joker in us comes out, but when others expect us to be serious, the jokes just don't seem to flow as easily.

It boils down to an important truth. We are naturally compelled to believe what others believe and to fulfill their expectations of us. This means that our closest circle of friends and family are forever in the process of calling us up to a new standard, or pulling us back down to the old one.

***We are compelled to believe what others believe and to fulfill their expectations of us.***

## They Shape Our Definition of "Normal"

Our perceptions change based on what we see most. We look into our own small piece of the world, project it to a global scale and call it normal. Then, because normal feels good, we become like whatever we see.

One interesting study published in the New England Journal of Medicine found that obesity, which obviously is not a bug you can catch, spreads from one person to another in a contagious like manner.[4] Investigators evaluated a "densely interconnected social network" of more than 12,000 people over the course of thirty-two years. They discovered that when a person becomes obese, his or her friend's chance of becoming obese increases by a whopping 57 percent.

How does this happen? According to Dr. Nicholas Christakis, the lead investigator, "You change your idea of what is an acceptable body type by looking at the people around you." Put simply, as our friends gain weight, we put on more pounds. Lifestyle choices that are common throughout the group, such as food choices and exercise avoidance, are what cause the weight gain. However, their disinterest or inability to create change was because their growing waistlines looked the same as everyone else's.

This desire for normalcy is working everywhere in our lives. Friends who overspend, work eighty hours a week, complain about their spouse or practice infidelity all influence us to do the same. They alter our definition of "normal", and then we live out that new definition. If you want to change your life direction, you need to join others who are already going that way.

***If you want to change your life direction, you need to join others who are already going that way.***

**Now Look Out**

If you're serious about changing your stories and your life, then you need to take a hard look at the people closest to you. It doesn't mean completely eliminating loved ones from your life, but it may mean reducing your exposure to them. It might also require finding new friends. Here are a few methods to consider.

*Method #1: Gather Your Friends*

It's important that you begin to separate your co-conspirators from the real friends who support you. Your social circle may include both, but only one type will help you reach your goals. Co-conspirators are those who participate in your unhealthy habits and keep you focused on the wrong things. They might mean well, but they are perpetuating the problem.

You need friends who have a vested interest in your vision. They are the people who encourage you when you fall, support your good choices and celebrate the life you want to live. They are the ones who raise your standards, keep you accountable to your goals and help to reset your definition of normal.

Gathering friends doesn't mean that you have to be drastic.

Try telling a few people about your goals and how important they are to you. Ask them to become supporters who will cheer you on, keep you focused on the positives and even join you on the journey. Paying lip service to your new life choices is great, but make sure that the actions of your professing friends line up with their words.

*Method #2: Join Your Comrades*

In addition to friends, you need comrades who are fighting the same fight. They may have different reasons, but they're playing the game to win. Getting results matters to them and they expect the same from you.

There is tremendous power in joining a group that is actively fighting a common enemy. Bruce Hood discusses this in his book, *The Self Illusion*. In it he writes, "You do not lose your identity but form a new one to address the group concern, of which you are now a member." Our self-image expands to include the collective desires and beliefs of the group.

Recall from chapter one, the power of Christmas for the WWI fighters. For the sake of a common story that deeply mattered to them, they temporarily ceased war and celebrated together. They discovered a common identity that dramatically changed their behaviour. We can use that same principle to our advantage.

Look for a pre-existing group that focuses on solving your exact problem. If there isn't one locally, find an online support group or create your own. Ask friends and family who have a common desire to join a weekly small group. As you do, your sense of self will integrate itself with the group and you will be more compelled to make the right choices.

*Method #3: Enlist Your Coaches*

Coaches are those who give you the tools and advice you need to take you from where you are to where you want to go. Many people think they can achieve their goals on their own, and some manage just fine. There are millions of resources, like books and websites, but few things close the gap faster than a personal coach.

First, coaches help you work through specific issues and answer questions that may take hours or days of research on your own. Second, they help create a custom plan of action that is unique to your situation. Third, they provide emotional support and motivation in a way that only human relationships can offer.

Your coach doesn't need to be a wise sage that knows all things. He or she just needs to know the answers to your current problem. It might be a friend who overcame the same issue, a local businessperson who knows the ropes, or a financial advisor or nutritionist who is a trained professional. Coaches come in all price ranges, from free to thousands of dollars. Whether or not you can afford the highest paid option doesn't matter, because there is someone out there who is willing and able to help you.

## LOOKING AROUND

The last external force to consider is your physical environment. Many of us fail to recognize it, but everything around us influences our thoughts and feelings. In short, your physical space tells a story.

***Your physical space tells a story.***

### Moved By Our Senses

We are moved by the world around us because the objects within it are speaking to each of our senses. From your eyes to your nose and ears, every part of you is being told a story. A cluttered home, for instance, says to your eyes, "I'm too overwhelmed!" The old "junk food" box in the kitchen might be flipping on the overwhelming desire to binge. The television in your workspace may be convincing you of your "need" to relax and not finish the project. All of these visual cues can hurt you and your goals.

Picture your living room or bedroom and everything it contains. Does anything stand out as especially significant? Are there gifts from past relationships, clothes from when you weighed more or items that promote or celebrate your old bad habits? You may be fond of your stuff, but you have to be careful that it does not sabotage you or set you up to fail. When a possession keeps your past mistakes on the forefront of your mind, it is better to throw it away.

Your senses of smell and hearing are moving you, too. The cravings you feel as you drive by a bakery is an obvious example for the nose, but it gets far more interesting than that. For instance, researchers have found that the aroma of cleaning products can promote generosity and fairness.[5] So you can make a completely different life choice just because the room smells fresher today? Yes! Your brain associates smells with attitudes and behaviours in unexpected ways.

Sounds, as it turns out, are just as influential. You are likely familiar with using music to calm down or wake up, but have you ever felt irritated by noise in the background? Don Campbell and Alex Doman, authors of *Healing at the Speed of Sound*, discovered through their work that, "Empty sound—the noise of a coffee grinder or of traffic outside—consists of a chaotic pattern of sound waves that, when interacting with your auditory system, cause your brain and body to respond in chaotic ways." As you can see, your nose and ears do more than just detect what's going on. They influence how you think, feel and behave.

I don't expect you to walk around your house and determine how each and every item is affecting you. What's important is that you acknowledge the fact that your physical space is speaking. As you go throughout your day, be aware of how you think and feel differently in different environments. Just as your body can respond to foods, your thoughts and emotions respond to all kinds of environmental cues. It is critical that you design your space with how you want to think and feel in mind.

***Your thoughts and emotions respond to all kinds of environmental cues.***

## Moved By Messages

We are bombarded by outside messages every single day. Our brains, using what are known as mirror neurons, reproduce in us what we see in our physical environment. For example, if you watch an Olympian run the 100-meter dash on television, your brain fires as though you are running the same race. According to psychologist Lydia Ievleva, author of *Imagine: Using mental imagery to reach your full potential*, watching professionals play a sport can prime you to perform better as well. On the flipside, watching someone play poorly will hurt your game. In both cases, your brain is reproducing what it sees.

You receive messages from everywhere: music, movies, television, radio and advertisements. All of them are trying to produce a thought, an emotion and many times, a specific action. If we are continually observing, reproducing and responding to our environment, then we need to ask: "What am I giving to my mirror neurons?"

It is important that you select your outside messages based on what you want to believe, desire or acquire in your life. Something will always fill your mental space, so find ways to take in the right messages as often as possible. Fill your life with things that represent and support your vision so you can mirror your way to victory.

***Select your outside messages based on what you want to believe, desire or acquire in your life.***

## Moved By Circumstance

Circumstances are yet another invisible force that affects how we think, feel and act. They influence our behaviour in ways we often don't anticipate, by activating and creating beliefs.

### *Circumstances Activate Stories*

We are multi-dimensional. William James, a leading American philosopher and psychologist in the late nineteenth century, argued that we all have more than one part to our personality. In *The Principles of Psychology*, James wrote, "a man has as many social selves as there are individuals who recognize him and carry an image of him in their mind."

These different parts of ourselves come out based on whom we are around at the time. Work colleagues may know you to be serious and professional, close friends get to see your funny side and your children think you're a mean dictator that won't let them do what they want. Bring your kids to work with you or meet your boss while out with your friends and they may question who you really are!

We may choose how we want to act in these various social settings, but something deeper gets the final say. For example, a person can be outgoing and talkative with friends, but quiet and reserved around new people because it activates feelings of shyness. Despite the immense desire to be more outgoing, this "I'm in danger" response makes it difficult to think of things to say or to work up the courage to speak.

It can be confusing and frustrating when different sides of our personalities come out. We get used to something about ourselves, but then a circumstance comes along and we can't believe how we acted. Have you ever asked yourself, "What's wrong with me?" as you walked away from some kind of blow-up, meltdown or devious behaviour?

Perhaps you feel compelled to lie and cover your tracks whenever things go wrong at work, but you wouldn't dream of ever lying to your spouse, regardless of the consequence. You might make healthy food choices whenever you go out to a restaurant, but when you're home alone, you can't stop indulging in fattening treats. You may struggle to fight the urge to drink when you're out with colleagues, but you have no desire to do it anywhere else. These contrasting behaviours can make you feel like a multitude of different people, wearing any number of different masks and wondering if the real you will ever come out. Rest assured that you are not a fraud. Rather, you have a series of contrasting selves.

Dr. Allen McConnell, a social psychologist and professor, has conducted extensive research on what he calls "self-aspects". According to McConnell, "the self-concept [is] a collection of multiple, context-dependent selves" that "at any given moment, a variety of contextual inputs (eg. environmental settings, social interactions, mental stimulus) serve to activate relevant self-aspects, which in turn organize [our] ongoing experiences and direct [our] actions."[6]

In other words, a situation triggers a self-aspect (e.g. friend), which contains its own unique set of stories, characteristics, feelings and behaviours. To make this easier to understand, here is my own example inside of Dr. McConnell's framework. Each of Dave's self-aspects (husband, friend, employee and student) has related attributes that influence how he acts in any given situation. When with his wife, Dave feels handsome, generous, kind and funny. At the office, however, he is typically only one of those things: funny. Otherwise, he is likely to be assertive, creative, persistent and quick-tempered.

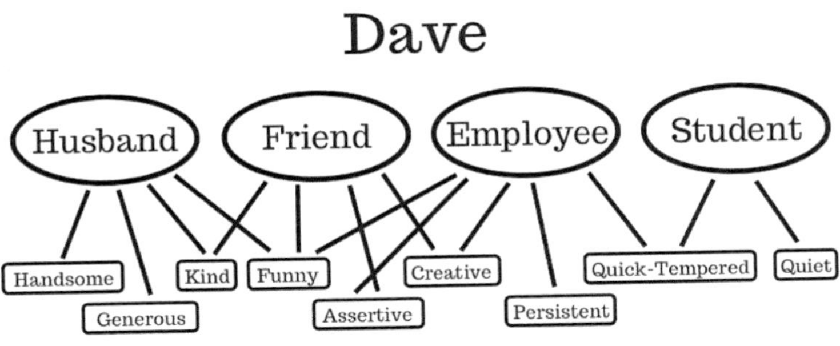


The truth is, we don't see the world through a permanent sense of self or set of beliefs. Yes, we have universal stories, but they aren't all active at the same time. Sometimes we feel confident, free and loving, while other times we feel afraid, restricted and closed off. Why? Our current environment sets the stage and calls upon whichever part of our personality seems best. Then we see the world through that state, give it a meaning and respond.

When the situation changes, we do too.

***We have universal stories, but they aren't all active at the same time.***

You may be a high performer at work, and yet go to another company in the same role and suddenly begin to struggle. Why? The new situation—new people, new team dynamics, new expectations and a new comfort zone—all make you feel, think and act differently. Your strengths, weaknesses and core beliefs are expressed differently because of a new situation.

Our actions are often a symptom of our current mental and emotional state. Beyond behaving differently, I bet you have different thoughts and feelings when you're around your old party friends than you do when you're with a mentor or another person you admire. The same is true when surrounded by people who love you versus when you're with strangers. How about when your favourite junk foods, or the treats you used to eat with your parents, are right in front of you? Different beliefs, values, worldviews and pathways rise to the surface, depending on what's happening around you.

Here is the key takeaway. Your personality comes out in relation to your environment. While you need to write new stories, you also need to create situations that "turn them on".

***While you need to write new stories, you also need to create situations that "turn them on".***

*Circumstances Change Stories*

With enough consistency, our circumstances have the power to either change us or keep us the same. The above mentioned Dr.

McConnell has found that our "self-aspects vary in their accessibility, with some self-aspects being more accessible (and thus, more likely to guide behavior) because of recent or frequent use." It seems that whatever part of your personality you activate most, is the one that becomes most dominant throughout your life.

If you want to believe something new, then you need to activate it as often as possible. On the other hand, if you decide to remain in your old environment and situations, which have supported your poor choices, then expect your old stories to keep plaguing you.

New persistent circumstances support change because they create an ongoing demand. When the demand disappears, we switch over to the path of least resistance. This could be whatever is most expected by others, what feels easiest (habit) or is most likely to produce a positive pain-free outcome. As you go through the work to create new beliefs, you need to be sure that they last. Choose circumstances that support and require your new beliefs and behaviours so they can become second nature.

***Choose circumstances that support and require your new beliefs.***

## Now Look Around

You can reinforce the truth about yourself and keep your focus and energy on track. How? By taking charge of your environment and circumstances. Here are three ways to put this new information to use.

*Method #1: Shape Your Space*

What kind of physical environment or objects would help communicate the truth back to you? Does a successful businessperson have a messy house? Does a person who values family have only a couple pictures of family somewhere in the basement? How would a person who already believes what you want to believe shape his or her personal space?

**How would a person who already believes what you want to believe shape his or her personal space?**

Next, determine what items in your environment might be sabotaging you. These are things that trigger unhealthy thoughts, feelings or actions. Maybe it's a bowl of candy in your office or a wine rack at home. It could even be your chosen route home from work, going by your favourite bakery or old drinking hole. Search out what moves you in the wrong direction and find ways to eliminate or avoid it.

Finally, add new items to your space that will keep you focused on victory. It could be a picture that embodies your vision and keeps reminding you that it's worth the fight. Or it may be something that reminds you of your spouse or family, so they are more often on your mind. It doesn't matter what it is, as long as it helps to keep you on track and focused on the truth of your new stories.

### *Method #2: Choose Your Ingredients*

What messages should you remove from your life? Is there music you should cut, movies you should avoid or magazines you should stop scanning at the checkout? It's not about being rigid. It's about being smart and supportive. We need to be picky about everything we consume, which means selecting only the best messages that align with what we want to believe and achieve.

Now what can you add to your life? Consider watching documentaries that inspire you, reading books that educate you and listening to music that motivates you to act. Fill your senses, your mind and your heart with the messages that will convince you of the truth and move you to victory.

### *Method #3: Set Up Your Circumstances*

In order to create real change, you must become the director of your own circumstances. Here are two steps to make it happen.

#### Step 1: Create Supportive Situations

We grow because of pressure. Muscle and bone get stronger because of stress, and so does our sense of self. Seek ways to place demands, restrictions and accountability on yourself that will require a new behaviour. Create new references and build new beliefs by forcing yourself out from your comfort zone to do what you know is necessary.

Try committing to something publically. For example, book a public speaking engagement or join an organization, like Toast Masters or Weight Watchers, that applies social pressure to make good choices. Embrace a bit of stress in your life, and let the positive tension push you in the right direction.

Not all situations, however, need to be challenging or stressful to help create change. What brings out the best in you? When, where or with whom is your willpower strongest? Does certain music bring you back to a more empowered state? Pay attention to the times when you are at your best and use what you learn to improve yourself in tough situations.

Step 2: Avoid Unsupportive Situations

Are there specific people, places, things or events that put you into a negative and disempowered frame of mind? One moment you're feeling great and the next you're ready for defeat. For some reason, you suddenly feel uncomfortable, anxious, insecure, angry or unresourceful. As you begin your process of change, it's better to walk away from or avoid these environments and circumstances that call upon the part of you that is less able to do what matters.

When are you at your worst? Is it when driving by bakeries, bars or malls? Is it after watching certain kinds of movies or listening to music that puts you on edge? Maybe it's after eating certain foods that make you feel tired and irritable. Choose to be aware of when you are most likely to experience your old stories or give in to poor choices. The more you separate yourself from them, the easier it becomes to change.

**Up Next**

First you felt the pain to wake up and then embraced hope to ensure you keep moving. Next, you aligned your outer forces to remove the roadblocks to change and support the inner shift you want to create. Now it's time for the final step: to Live on Purpose. You have the power to defeat the stories that weaken you and make permanent the ones that serve you. So if you're ready, let's dive right in.

# Chapter 14
# Step 4 - Live On Purpose: Making New Stories Permanent

You were made to win, not to battle helplessly against impossible forces that keep pushing you into poor choices and bad circumstances. You can be set free from the impulsive demands of physical appetites, from emotional wounds and from whatever else is holding you back. However, living in that freedom is a choice and it takes determination and practice.

It all comes down to your focus and choices. Your brain's wiring adapts to whatever occupies your mind and directs your actions on a daily basis. The choice is yours to reset your thinking and create new desires and impulses. You can continue to live in the same old bad habits, or you can embrace your freedom as a co-author of your own stories.

***Your brain's wiring adapts to whatever occupies your mind and directs your actions on a daily basis.***

Let's briefly summarize the first three steps before diving into the final one. First, pain alerts you to a problem and brings you out of faulty stories so truth can tear them down. Second, hope pulls you forward towards something of value so you don't stay back and rebuild the same old comfortable walls. Third, supportive outer forces minimize the internal resistance you feel and help to indoctrinate you with healthy new stories.

Now there's only one thing left to do: Live On Purpose. This final step is about taking responsibility for your life. Everything you think, say, do and focus on can create new stories and make them permanent. But first, let's begin with a formula.

## The iREAP Heart Change Formula

In the Life is Story chapter, I explained that beliefs come from experiences and the meanings we assign to them. Thankfully, that's not the only source. Through the practice of mindfulness and deliberate thought and action, we have the power to erase old beliefs and write new ones.

Through my own research and experience, I have combined several principles to create a simple heart change formula. If you want to develop a new set of beliefs, then you need to sow the right seeds and take the right steps to make sure they grow and reap a harvest in your life. That's why I call it the iREAP Heart Change Formula.

**Information x (Repetition + Engagement + Alignment + Proof) = New Belief**

### *Wear Out with* REPETITION

Sheer repetition has incredible power. Dr. Shad Helmstetter is a well-known behavioural researcher and best selling author with expertise in personal growth and motivational psychology. In his book *What to Say When You Talk to Your Self*, Helmstetter writes, "The brain simply believes what you tell it most."

This insight into repetition seems basic, but in reality, many of us tend to overlook it. Changing a belief requires repetition so that it can take root and become relevant. However, this doesn't mean that lots of positive affirmations will transform you. In fact, according to Dr. Alexander Loyd, author of *The Healing Codes*, speaking positive affirmations when you don't believe them can actually cause more harm than good. When you say something that conflicts with a heart belief, your body produces a stress response. The subconscious mind is a natural lie detector that causes a physical reaction when you speak against what it knows to be "the truth".

For example, if you tell yourself that you are beautiful, smart or wealthy when your heart has determined the exact opposite to be true, you accomplish nothing. The only result is stress, anxiety and an even stronger wall around the unhealthy story. Repetition is a good start, but new information needs more to become a healthy new belief.

### *Overwhelm with* ENGAGEMENT

A lot of life runs on autopilot. Our Reticular Activating System and Confirmation Bias, discussed in the first chapter, ignore most of what happens around us and reject everything that conflicts with what we currently believe. As a result, it's not easy to get new information in the door. However, when we engage ourselves in mind, emotions and body, we can exit from autopilot mode and facilitate a change of beliefs.

Engagement of the mind is a matter of focus, which I have

discussed at length. When we consistently focus on the truth, we alter the stories of our hearts and shift our habits and desires.

Next is emotion. Extreme levels, whether high or low, can bring about change by directing our attention and creating what seems like evidence of the truth. Consider the feelings of intense excitement or anxiety over something in the future. Although it hasn't happened yet, your brain has already assumed that it must be true.

In essence, your brain is saying, "This is true, therefore I must get excited." Interestingly, though, these assumptions also work in reverse. Your brain assumes that if one direction works (truth = excitement), then the opposite way must work as well (excitement = truth). So when an emotional experience comes knocking at the door with new information in hand, your brain says, "I'm emotional, therefore this must be true."

What about the physical component? Your body plays a supportive role in the engagement of your mind and emotions. According to Andrew Newberg, author of *How God Changes Your Brain*, how we move our bodies can alter our state of mind, reduce anxiety and depression, and help us focus on a singular object. When you engage your body, you empower your mind to reject distractions and zero in on the object of your attention.

How we move our bodies and use our voices also affects the way we feel. Stand up straight, take a deep breath and speak with confidence. These are just a few ways you can tell your brain to feel better. When you get up and move in a way that changes how you feel, you think more clearly and interpret new information in a more positive and empowering way.

You can build a compelling case for a new belief by engaging all of yourself in mind, emotions and body. In combination, they create a sense of certainty that your brain cannot reject or ignore. In this way, you can force the new story in.

***You can build a compelling case by engaging yourself in mind, emotions and body.***

*Sneak in with ALIGNMENT*

Your brain resists dramatically new information, but is quick to accept anything that fits with your current beliefs. Like a Trojan horse, you can use this fact to sneak in a transformational story, hidden within a welcoming package.

In other words, you can leverage alignment by connecting what you want to believe with something that you already do believe. For example, you can attach a new value to an existing one, or an empowering worldview to a healthier belief about yourself. Let's consider a few examples.

**A Value Within a Value**

Are you struggling to pay attention to your health? Connect it to need love for variety by finding more interesting ways to get active each day. You can also leverage connection and learning by signing up for a healthy cooking class with your spouse.

You may want to improve a relationship, but you have more of a task-oriented personality. While it doesn't mean you can't care about connection, it does mean you have a more difficult time remembering to make it a priority. Use your achievement value by setting tactical goals like how many phone calls you make or dates you go on together. Make it a mini game and celebrate each victory along the way.

In both examples, you are sneaking in a new value by focusing on what you currently care about most. In the first example, you are training your brain to get excited for variety, connection and learning (current values) when you think about health (new value). In the second example, it anticipates achievement (current) when spending time on relationships (new).

**A Worldview Within a Worldview**

An unhelpful worldview can really hold you back in life. However, you can choose to shift your focus to a supportive story that you already believe. When you do this, the negative worldview loses its power and you become able to make better choices. Let's look at an example.

It can be difficult to say no to the people you care about because it feels like you're withholding your love from them. For a parent who feels this way, a personal story may say, "Good parents always give their kids what they want." You can battle this conflict by focusing on something better, such as, "A healthy child has healthy boundaries."

As you can see, you may believe that you should give your kids what they want, but if you also believe that children need boundaries, you now have a place in which to hook the new story. If boundaries are a good thing, then maybe kids *do* need to hear no from time to time. Instead of resisting and fighting with an old worldview, you found a way to sneak in a new one.

**An Identity Within a Worldview**

Is your sense of self a little shaky right now? You may be at a low point or find yourself struggling with stories that have plagued you for years. Either way, you can sometimes sidestep those limitations by appealing to an empowering worldview.

What do I mean? Let's presume you believe you're not smart enough to take on a leadership role at work. When you think about more responsibility and the demands of being in charge, you cringe and hope someone else will step up to the plate.

However, if you believe a law of life that proves your situation is possible, you won't have to feel so afraid. For example, consider the truth, "People get better with practice" or, "All things are possible for those who believe." You may not feel fully prepared right now, but this better perspective lets you approach leadership as a set of skills you merely need to develop.

In essence, you can allow your sense of self to grow by first believing that it's possible. You do this by removing your focus from the limitations of your self-image and looking to a bigger worldview that supports you.

**A Worldview Within an Identity**

Just as you can expand your identity with an empowering worldview, you can shift your worldview with a healthy identity. For example, you may be struggling to find or

> have faith for the resources you need to build your business or ministry. After hitting roadblock after roadblock, you're finding it impossible to believe the resources you need are actually out there for you.
>
> What if instead of focusing on the apparent lack in the world, you chose to remember that you are a resourceful person who stands in the blessing of God? Of course you still need to put in the effort, but now you can be re-inspired to go for it.
>
> By doing this, you take a giant step from a disempowering worldview to a supportive identity and make room to believe something better about your situation. Now you can see abundance in the world again, because your sense of self has opened the door to it.

I could go on with other examples, but here is the key: start with what you already believe. Alignment allows you to use an empowering belief to shift your focus and create a wedge in a lie that disempowers you. It pokes holes in your negative assumptions and sets up your heart and mind to receive something new.

***Alignment allows you to shift your focus and create a wedge in a lie that disempowers you.***

*Overrule with* PROOF

As irrational as the brain can be at times, it is fully willing to change if you give it enough reasons. It isn't satisfied with just good intentions, positive affirmations or hopeful wishes alone. It wants cold, hard facts that prove what you have believed is a lie and what you want to believe now is the truth. If you can give your own brain enough evidence, you can convince it of just about anything.

### Putting It into Practice

With the iREAP Heart Change Formula in mind, it's time for practical application. Through focus and action, you can transform your stories and your life. Each method in the following pages uses different parts of the formula to produce a change. So read them through to discover which ones might be right for you.

## THINK ON PURPOSE

The mind is one of our most precious resources, but it can also be a horrible enemy. In today's world of overstimulation, our thought lives are running away on us. We are feeling distracted by our long lists of responsibilities and defeated by negative thoughts that don't seem to stop. As a result, we keep ourselves stuck in old patterns and held back by defeating stories. We need to take our focus back.

When you learn to harness the power of your mind, everything can change. By managing your thoughts, you are more able to govern your beliefs and live a more effective and fulfilling life. Here are four methods that you can use, starting now, to take every thought captive and get your mind back on the right side.

### Think Method #1: Notice Your Thoughts & Feelings

It's easy to get so caught up in the busyness of life that we lose track of the steady dialogue going on inside of our minds. We think thousands of thoughts each day and, not surprisingly, a lot of them are on repeat. Your ability to remain aware of what your mind is saying can have a big impact on what you believe.

You may decide on the new story, "Wealthy people can be just as humble as the poor" and be fully ready to believe it. However, because of old habitual thinking, you continue to silently complain about the wealthier people around you. Your ongoing narrative is competing with your new worldview story and, as a result, the shift isn't able to stick. The competing stories keep you stuck.

Paul said, "Whatever is true, whatever is honorable, whatever is right, whatever is pure, whatever is lovely, whatever is of good repute, if there is any excellence and if anything worthy of praise, dwell on these things" (Philippians 4:8). In other words, he was saying to only allow our minds to think about things that empower us. Why? Because he knew that what we think about most is what directs our hearts and our lives. When we allow our minds to run wild, we leave our stories up to chance.

***When we allow our minds to run wild, we leave our stories up to chance.***

If you struggle in this area, try going on a mental positivity diet. Every time you notice yourself slipping into a negative pattern, get up and move your body, shift your focus to something new or change the story you are telling to something more positive. You have the power to tell your brain what to think.

Try this three-step model to keep your mind on track.

*Step 1: See It*

Noticing your thoughts takes practice. It's so easy to let your mind run wild that you don't even listen to the conversation. In fact, many of our thoughts are automatic and all but ignored.

Decide on a trigger to prompt a check-in with yourself. For

example, every time you flip a light switch, get a text message or take a sip of water, stop and ask, "Are my thoughts empowering?" In addition, whenever you feel yourself getting negative, stop, take a deep breath and ask, "What story am I telling myself?"

*Step 2: Shift It*

A lot of our negative thinking is so habitual that when we try to think about something else, we quickly jump back to the very thing we're trying to avoid. When you notice a negative line of thinking, you may need to do more than just decide to think about something else.

Shift the moment you're in by moving your body, adjusting your breathing and changing the way you feel. You can even visualize pushing the thought away or hitting it with a sledgehammer. When I have a nagging thought, I imagine putting it into a box and I kick it into outer space. As unusual as it sounds, it works for me.

*Step 3: Swap It*

Now that you feel better, your mind is ready for a new thought. Choose to look at your circumstance in a more empowering way. Tell yourself a truthful and supportive story that lifts you up and positions you for success.

**Think Method #2: Search for Evidence of Past Success**

The sad reality is that most of us are much better at finding our faults than our successes. When we do something good, we may enjoy it for a few minutes, but then quickly move on to the next thing. But when we do something we deem to be bad, we criticize ourselves and focus on it for the rest of the day or week.

Here is an important principle. Your past is a well from which you drink each day. Fill it with positive memories and it will nourish you with confidence and hope. Fill it with negative ones and it will drain you of what you need to succeed.

To believe your new stories, you must find evidence that they might be true. If your well is full of memories of failure and bad past events, your mind will work hard to reject the truth. You need to actively search your past for times when you lived according to a higher identity, value, worldview or pathway. Instead of reliving the "bad" moments, which we all have, choose to recall and focus on the good. They are there if you are willing to look. And when you do, you can use the discovery to start breaking down the lies.

***To believe your new stories, you must find evidence that they might be true.***

Take a moment to write down your new story as well as all of the times in your life you lived as though it was true. Go back in your mind's eye and experience each of those events again. Remember how good it felt, celebrate it and let it become proof of the real you.

## Think Method #3: Gain New Knowledge and Skills

Education and skill building support the tactical side of goal achievement, but that's not all they do. Faulty stories are the false assumptions we made because we didn't know any better at the time. They still feel true because they are rooted in ignorance. However, we can make a change by breaking free from our lack of understanding and ability.

***Faulty stories feel true as long as they remain rooted in ignorance.***

You may believe that it's impossible to lose weight with your health condition or genetic predisposition. Perhaps you assume that you're too old to go back to school or to start a business. Are you sure? We live in an information-rich world. The instruction and inspiration you need is really just a few clicks away. You don't have to follow the exact systems as other people, but you do need to challenge your thinking by learning something new and discovering what others have done in similar situations.

Learning also helps to increase self-efficacy. Many people feel stuck because they believe they are unable to act or that they don't have what it takes. If you think that you will never lose weight because you don't know how or that it's just too hard, then you aren't likely to act. You have accepted defeat before the start and adopted a story of helplessness that prevents you from accomplishing your goals.

You can, however, overcome this negative thinking by developing your skills and learning what you don't know. Start by reading books, attending seminars, speaking with experts or listening to the success stories of those who have overcome your problem. Suddenly you feel more confident to get up and take action. There is no more second-guessing or making silly mistakes because you now know what's right and wrong. As your self-efficacy increases, your sense of control moves from external (happening *to* you) to internal (happening *with* you), and your story changes from, "I can't do this" to "I know I can."

### Think Method #4: Direct Your Daily Attention

Let me remind you just one more time of what Dr. Andrew Newberg said: "The more you focus on something—whether that's math or auto racing or football or God—the more that becomes your reality, the more it becomes written into the neural connections of your brain."

King David seemed to be on the same page as Dr. Newberg. In the first Psalm, he wrote, "How blessed is the man who does not walk in the counsel of the wicked, nor stand in the path of sinners, nor sit in the seat of scoffers" (Psalm 1:1). According to David, the blessed man does not follow along with sinful instruction, nor does he actively sin of his own accord.

So what is this man's secret? Continuing in the next verse, we find out: "But his delight is in the law of the LORD, and in His law he meditates day and night" (Psalm 1:2). The only thing this man is doing to guard himself is consistent meditation on God's word. By doing so, God's truth is wired into his brain to shape his beliefs, standards and sense of reality.

What we focus on each and every day matters. The music we listen to, the movies we watch and the conversations we participate in all have an effect on how we think, feel and live. Just like what you eat is used to construct the cells of your body, the things you think about construct your reality. A structured plan of daily meditation will have a major impact on the stories you adopt and the choices you make.

***Just like what you eat is used to construct the cells of your body, the things you think about construct your reality.***

The truth is, you already practice meditation, but chances are it's not working to your benefit. To be clear, I'm not referring to the modern practice of emptying your mind. Rather, I mean deep focus and reflective thought.

Benjamin Franklin put this principle into use with his system of moral perfection. He decided early in his adult life that he wanted to be a man of strong character. After determining which virtues were the most important to develop, he divided them into a list of thirteen: temperance, silence, order, resolution, frugality, industry, sincerity, justice, moderation, cleanliness, tranquility, chastity and humility.

Franklin then assigned one week to each virtue, creating a thirteen-week block that he repeated four times in a year. Throughout each week, he focused on a single virtue, taking notes during the day of every time he failed. For example, if he was on humility week and caught himself being conceited, he marked it down for later review. Every evening, he was able to evaluate his progress and consider what he could do to improve.

This system, and others like it, works because it uses repetition and the mental engagement of deep thought. Dr. Caroline Leaf, a researcher of the human brain and best-selling author, explains in her book *Switch On Your Brain*, that deep thinking helps the brain to rewire itself. Whatever problems that have been wired into our thinking can, according to Dr. Leaf, be wired right back out of it.

***Whatever problems that have been wired into our thinking can be wired right back out.***

Thinking deeply seems to have gone out of style. Everything today seems urgent, so our minds bounce from one thing to the next. We rarely take the time to engage our minds and meditate on the things that will improve our reality and empower our lives. Even when we do have down time, we get restless and find ways to distract ourselves through television, music, games and idle chitchat.

Here are five steps to take back control and apply the power of strategic attention.

*Step 1: Choose Your Stories*

Identify the Identity, Values, Worldview and Pathways that you have selected as your new stories. Put them all in order of importance, with those that will make the greatest impact on your vision at the top. You only want to focus on one at a time, so assign at least one to two weeks exclusively to each story. Now you have your full focus schedule.

*Step 2: Schedule the Time*

Taking time for quiet contemplation can feel like a waste when you're not used to it. Start by scheduling 15 to 30 minutes first thing in the morning and immediately before bed. If you need to get up a little earlier and go to bed a little later, then so be it. It's important to start the day off with the right focus and to give your brain something to digest while you sleep.

Next, schedule three-minute blocks of time throughout the day to check in with yourself and evaluate how you're doing. It can be at the top of every hour, or every time you eat or take a drink. In these moments, ask yourself, "Am I living this week's story?"

*Step 3: Think Strategically*

It's easy to sit and think without getting much out of it, so be strategic. During your scheduled quiet time, take your new story and unpack it, so it can become second nature to you. Here are some suggestions:

- DEFINE it – What does the dictionary say about it? What is your own personal definition?
- EXPLORE it – Why is this story of such personal significance to you? Why does it matter to others? Why does it matter to your vision? How will it make your life better?
- LEARN about it – What book can you read on the subject? What scripture is of relevance? What audio message will help?
- JOURNAL it – Take a single statement from a book, a Bible verse or any of these suggested questions and put it at the top of a page. Now write out exactly what it means to you and why it is important.
- PRAY it – Make it a matter of prayer and ask God to help you.
- USE it – How can you put it in use today? How can you make it a subject of contemplation for the day? Who can you discuss it with today?
- EVALUATE it – How did you do in this area today? In what ways did you fail and how will you do better next time?

*Step 4: Think Vividly*

Take it to the next level by engaging all of your senses through mental imagery. You have the ability to choose what scene plays in your mind at any given time. According to Dr. Caroline Leaf in her book *Switch On Your Brain*, "rehearsing things mentally is a great everyday example of how you can think and more deeply reflect on daily actions. Each time you do this, you change the memory." She goes on to explain that every time you practice that mental image, "the newly built memory becomes increasingly stronger".

This is precisely what we are doing in developing new stories. We are changing and crafting memories in a way that supports us. Are you ready to turn each new story into a clear mental image? Here are some questions to get you thinking:

- Assuming you believed this empowering truth, how would you know? In what scenarios would you live differently?
- How would you act if you truly believed your new identity, values, worldview and pathways?
- Think of someone who clearly believes what you want to believe. What choices would they make?

The objective here is to create a scenario that you can watch unfold like a movie. Your brain is slow to distinguish imagination from reality, so the more you can experience the imagery, the better it will work. You are, in effect, creating healthy new memories from the safety of your home.

***You are creating healthy new memories from the safety of your home.***

The key is to use as many senses as possible.

- SEE the people and places in vivid colour and as much detail as you can.
- HEAR the voices, background noises and anything else

that is relevant.

- SMELL, TASTE & TOUCH anything notable within the environment.
- FEEL the physical and emotional sensations of the experience.

*Step 5: Celebrate the Win*

Create a positive connection between the actions and outcome you just visualized. Train your brain to expect positive feelings from taking those same actions in real life. To build this association, take time to feel, enjoy and celebrate your healthy choices and successful results, even if it is just imaginary.

***Train your brain to expect positive feelings from taking those same actions in real life.***

You also need to reward yourself for following through on your daily plan. Even if mental imagery wasn't used, you still want to create an association for your brain that you're doing something wonderful. At the end of each session, remind yourself of the ultimate vision and celebrate the progress you just made.

## ACT ON PURPOSE

The most effective way to change or create a belief is through an experience. After all, it was your past experiences and their meanings that led to your current set of stories in the first place. Now, through deliberate and consistent action, you can change them.

The bottom line is, the more you experience something, the more natural and believable it becomes. Your conscious choices, focus and repetition all rewire your brain and what you think is true. You have the power to rewrite your stories by acting on purpose. You can believe whatever you want to believe by living as though you already do.

***You can believe whatever you want to believe by living as though you already do.***

### Act Method #1: Declare with Full Engagement

Let's look at our Psalm 1 meditation key one more time. The Hebrew word *hagah*, used for meditation, has more than one definition. It also means to declare, utter, growl, moan, groan and roar. Clearly, the power of meditation is not just found in quiet inner thoughts. We can take it up a notch with the full engagement of our body and emotions.

You can increase the power of the words you speak by choosing an emotional state that best represents them. For example, groaning and moaning would link sorrow and pain to whatever you say. Growling connects it with anger, while roaring attaches it to certainty, confidence and power.

***Increase the power of your words by choosing an emotional state that best represents them.***

When we align our words with our emotions and our physiology, we can't help but influence our beliefs. Tony Robbins, a best selling author and popular life coach, believes these declarations are so powerful because they have the ability to activate the right beliefs and to eliminate the faulty ones. According to Tony, "what you consistently speak with emotional intensity, you will experience, you will create and you will become. The words that you speak with enough emotional conviction become the life you live."[1]

Start using the power of declarations with the following steps.

*Step 1: Craft Your Declaration*

Choose your words wisely. Remember that positive affirmations can, at times, create more stress and harm than good. So as you craft your declaration, see how it feels. If certain words cause anxiety, then switch them to something that aligns with your current beliefs a little more. For example, instead of saying, "I am beautiful," try "I am loved by a God who says I am beautiful. Every day I see more and more of what He sees." Focusing on the act or process of becoming or believing your new story may be more effective for you at first.

Here is a declaration I created to help me move towards greater physical health and fitness. The words I chose may seem empty, boring or over the top to you but that's ok, because they feel great to me! Notice that I include statements about myself (able, driven, passionate), my values (wisdom, health), my worldview (unlimited possibilities) and my pathway (make the right choices). All four stories are now pointing in one unified direction.

"I am a son of God, driven by purpose, fueled by passion and whole in spirit, soul and body. Everything in me is breaking through to abundant health and life. By God's grace, I am a co-author of my destiny, empowered to do all things in a world of unlimited possibilities. I am compelled to live wisely and to make healthy choices in everything I do. I am able; I am willing; I am unstoppable."

*Step 2: Choose Your State*

What emotional state best represents and supports the words

you're speaking? If you are declaring that you are becoming more and more receptive to love, then you likely want to feel a sense of confidence, peace and gratitude. If you are speaking of drive and a 'never quit' attitude, then choose tenacity, boldness and power.

You won't just enter the best emotional state because you want it. Rather, you must generate it with the words you speak, the mental images you project and the way you move your body.

### *Step 3: Move Congruently*

If you were absolutely convinced about what you are saying, how would you move your body? If, like above, you are becoming more and more receptive to love, then you likely don't need to stomp your feet and pound your chest. However, if you are speaking of drive and tenacity, then those actions are appropriate. The best place to start is with choosing your face, your posture and your movements.

Your face speaks volumes. Not just outwardly to other people, but also inwardly to your own brain. One interesting study[2] clearly reveals the effects of facial expressions on the way we feel. First, the participants who made a positive expression felt better, while those who made a negative one felt worse. Second, those who were more aware of how they felt and determined to understand themselves, responded even more powerfully. Third, creating visual feedback by looking at their expressions in the mirror also increased the effect. To summarize the findings, put on the facial expression that aligns with your words, pay attention to how you feel and watch yourself do it. These three things will make a big difference in shifting your state.

The way you stand is also important. Research shows that

standing tall with your head up and shoulders back can alter the hormonal balance in your body and make you feel more powerful and confident. Social psychologist Amy Cuddy explained how this works in her popular Ted Talk entitled, *Your Body Language Shapes Who You Are.* She suggests that if we learn to make minor adjustments to our body language, "it could significantly change the way [our lives] unfold."

Finally, determine how you want to move your body. If you really believed what you were saying, what would it look like? Try talking with your hands, pumping your fist, clapping, jumping, cheering, laughing or spinning in carefree circles. It might feel really strange, but if these are the things you do when you are already feeling confident, then doing them when you aren't so sure can bring on the state of certainty that you need.

### *Step 4: Speak with Certainty*

If you really believed what you were saying, how would you say it? If you do it half-heartedly like a lame positive affirmation that you really don't believe, then don't even bother. Put some conviction behind your words and say it like you mean it!

### *Step 5: Feel it in Your Core*

This whole exercise is about creating certainty in your mind, emotions and body. You can recite a happy phrase all you want, but if you don't feel anything, then it's not fully engaging, and it's not going to make a meaningful difference.

Certainty and emotional intensity don't just happen. It's up to you to create the feelings you want. Can you feel the emotions that represent the words you're speaking? If you could watch me when

I'm home alone, you might think I'm crazy. I often go through my house, pacing and praying or just speaking. When I don't feel like it, I make the decision to pause what I'm doing and to focus on choosing a new supportive state. I tell myself to 'wake up and engage', I clap and I shout. Basically, I do whatever it takes to make myself feel what I want to feel in that moment.

***Certainty and emotional intensity don't just happen. It's up to you to create the feelings you want.***

Those who learn to master their states are better able to master their lives. We live from our feelings and consequently, we can either react to whatever happens in life or we can choose the feelings that will best serve us and then generate them ourselves. It's not an easy skill to develop, but in my experience, it's definitely worth it.

You may not feel much when you first start out with declarations, but again, there is power in repetition. Declare the words over and over again with enough engagement of your mind and body, and I can guarantee that you will begin to feel something. You can try using music that inspires you, and add additional emphasis to the words that mean the most to you if it helps. Do whatever it takes to feel the words you're declaring.

### Act Method #2: Prove Through Experiential Learning

While our stories and pathways came from experiences, we don't have to go digging through the past trying to find how we got them. Instead, we can simply choose to create new experiences that replace the old ones. According to our iREAP heart change formula, we are creating proof through action.

Imagine that you have a fear of public speaking. You believe you will lose your words, that others will judge you and that you will look and feel like a fool. These are all common self-defeating assumptions that usually don't have a lot of supporting evidence.

Regardless of the truth, though, they are real to you. That's why you feel such intense anxiety and dread every time you think about standing up in front of a crowd. It's a fear response that wants to protect you from a dangerous situation, but in reality, it's holding you back. This is where acting on purpose comes into play.

Fear is a common feeling, but just because it's common doesn't mean that it's supportive. In circumstances like this one, we need to face our fears and discomforts, and act anyway. As we do, we reclaim our authority to choose what we believe. Running from fear, on the other hand, causes it to intensify. There is simply no standing still with it. It is either increasing or decreasing, and it's up to us to decide.

Despite your fear to speak in public, you join a speaker's guild like Toast Masters. Your first speech is short, but scary. You prepare like crazy, practicing in front of a mirror until you have it down and you're ready to go. You stand in front of the small, supportive crowd a little shaky, as the words begin to flow from your mouth. You notice that people are nodding and smiling at you and you begin to feel a little more at ease. You tell a little joke and get some hearty laughter and your confidence grows even more. By the end of your short talk, you're feeling great and you even get an applause.

This new experience can now be used to break down your previous assumptions. You learned the truth by testing the lies and proving them wrong. It may take a few attempts, or you might have to start with baby steps, but through deliberate action, you can create new stories.

**_You can learn the truth by testing the lies and proving them wrong._**

Experiential learning also helps to pave new automatic pathways. As you go through the process of taking deliberate action every day, you weaken old habits while building new ones. The end result is a set of impulses that support your change efforts.

Follow these steps to prove yourself into a new story.

*Step 1: Choose Your Story*

Decide on the new story that you want to integrate into your life, along with its related lie if it has one.

*Step 2: Convert Truth to Action*

Your aim here is to accomplish two things: prove the lie is a lie and the truth is the truth. You are choosing to act as if you already are the person you want to be. In doing so, you force your heart and mind to catch up with the beliefs that your actions represent.

**_Force your heart and mind to catch up with the beliefs that your actions represent._**

The actions can be performed once in a while or every single day. While many of them will also be supportive in reaching your goals, their true purpose for now is to change what you believe and create new effortless pathways. Here are a few examples.

Identity Actions:

| I am… | Actions |
|---|---|
| Bold and courageous | Make a few extra sales calls without hesitation.<br>Stand up against an injustice that has been bothering you.<br>Approach a stranger to ask for the time.<br>Go skydiving, whitewater rafting or bungee jumping. |
| Active and vibrant | Schedule 10-minute walks throughout the day.<br>Do 15 minutes of stretching every morning.<br>Choose your favourite physical activity and join a group class with a friend. |
| Disciplined | Set aside 30 minutes every day for an activity that will move you towards your goal, and protect that time with your life.<br>Put yourself in mildly tempting circumstances and feel how good it is to say no.<br>Go to bed and wake up earlier. |

Value Actions:

| I value… | Actions |
|---|---|
| Acceptance | Actively find ways to include someone in your life who you have recently ignored or rejected.<br>Have a conversation with a person who lives a lifestyle you completely disagree with, but ignore what you dislike and choose to find three things you appreciate about him or her. |

| I value… | Actions |
|---|---|
| Compassion | Set aside an evening a week or month to volunteer at a soup kitchen.<br>Become a Big Brother or Big Sister to a young person who needs positive mentorship.<br>Live on the street for a few days (I have a friend who did this!) |
| Family | Make family dinner non-negotiable at least 3 nights a week.<br>Have a weekly date night with your spouse.<br>Go to your child's sporting event and be fully present without any work distractions. |

Worldview Actions:

| I believe… | Actions |
|---|---|
| Intelligence is grown. | Create a growth plan that includes taking a course, reading a book or attending a seminar.<br>Immediately teach what you learned to someone else and find a way to apply it to your life. |
| Wealth creates opportunity to be generous. | Make a plan to save 10% of your income.<br>Actively find ways to give to those in need. |
| Life is cause and effect. | Eat a healthy breakfast so you feel better through the day.<br>Set aside time every morning to work on your bigger projects and see your job as more manageable.<br>Respond differently to conflict and witness how things happen differently. |

Pathway Actions:

| I commit… | Actions |
|---|---|
| To never give up when I feel like quitting. | Set a goal to do something small, like read a page from a book, every single day. (Keeping it miniature makes it sustainable, but it still takes some effort.)<br>Start each day with your most difficult task. |
| If I speak up, then I will make a difference. | Join an organized group that fights for a cause that is close to your heart.<br>Speak to your boss about a problem you see, as well as the action you can take to solve it.<br>Share your opinion on a hot topic with your friends. |
| When I enter the kitchen, I will celebrate my progress. | Attach your before picture to the fridge, along with an image that represents your goal.<br>Whenever you enter the room, think about your healthy choices that day, say a prayer of thanksgiving, clap your hands or do a little dance. (The objective is to make yourself feel great without using food.) |

You have countless options when creating a learning experience. The only important measure of quality is that it makes a difference in what you believe. Ask yourself, "What do I need to have happen in order to question this lie and start to believe the truth?"

***"What do I need to have happen in order to question this lie and start to believe the truth?"***

Acting on purpose might require baby steps. If the thought of this exercise is filling you with anxiety, then take a sheet of paper and write the ultimate evidence of your new belief. Below it, write the next best thing, which is a little less difficult. Keep writing your list of progressively less difficult actions until you arrive at something that feels challenging, but doable.

For example, you may want to ask for a raise at work, but feel uncomfortable because you don't believe your true worth. Your progression might look like this:

1. Ask for a raise.
2. Go to a networking event and introduce myself to whoever I think is "too important" to want to know me.
3. Be a strong contributor in a meeting that includes my boss and other senior executives.
4. Ask someone I admire to be a mentor.
5. Ask for a free room upgrade the next time I check in at a hotel.
6. Tell my boss I can't work late.
7. Ask for a difficult work project that is outside of my comfort zone.
8. Tell a waiter I really didn't like the food.
9. Ask a friend to help with a home project that could require his or her whole weekend.
10. Graciously accept a compliment without saying anything but, "Thank you."

Whatever you need, choose your actions and put them in your schedule. You don't need to exhaust yourself, but you do need to be stretched and challenged. You won't change and grow if you don't push your limits.

***You won't change and grow if you don't push your limits.***

*Step 3: Mentally Prepare*

Pushing yourself is stressful because your brain likes to think it already has life all figured out. So when you take a step outside of your invisible boundaries, you feel threatened and scared. While it's almost always an empty threat, it sure feels real. Thankfully, you can soften the blow by preparing for action with mental imagery.

Imagine your action going exactly as you intended it to go. See, hear and feel it unfolding right in front of you. This step will reduce your stress by making you feel more capable, and it will increase your ability to succeed by practicing the tough choices.

*Step 4: Do It*

No need for explanation on this one. Stop planning and imagining, and just do it already!

*Step 5: Track & Define*

Your last step is to pay attention to how you feel throughout this process. Check in with yourself after each action. How do you feel about what happened? Was it really as bad as you expected? What evidence do you now have that the old belief was a lie? What evidence do you now have of the truth?

If the outcome wasn't good, then give it a meaning that empowers you. You stepped out and spoke to a stranger, but were promptly brushed off. Decide that the other person is having a bad day and that he or she may be struggling with fear, too. Never let a bad experience define you. Rather, choose to define it first.

***Never let a bad experience define you. Rather, choose to define it first.***

When the outcome is positive, embrace the positive feelings, take time to celebrate the victory and actively make the experience about you. Choose to define your win as meaning something great about who you are, what you value or how the world works.

The act of finding pleasure and giving meaning to little victories doesn't have to be restricted just to the things you schedule. Every time you feel good about something, create an association. When you practice self-awareness, you'll find these opportunities everywhere.

I'll give you an example of something that happened to me. It might seem small and insignificant on the surface, but I chose to take 30 seconds and make it a big deal. I was driving with my father and brother to my parents' cottage. It was a couple of days after Christmas and there had been a lot of snow so we needed to shovel the roof. We were already in the car and well on our way when I realized that my gloves were still wet on the inside from the day before.

We didn't have much time left, but I decided to take out the liners of the gloves, turn them inside out and put them on my knees by the air vent. As we made the turn onto the cottage road, I picked up the gloves and liners, put them back together and fastened the Velcro in much less time than I thought it would take.

While the process was more complicated than you might think, it wasn't that big of a deal and yet I felt great about it. I suddenly had a warm and glowing feeling about the whole experience and, rather than brushing it off as foolish, I chose to embrace it. I celebrated the fact that this little victory meant that I am resourceful, intelligent and dexterous. Does it sound like a bit much? Who cares! I decided I was worth telling an empowering story about something that made me feel good, and you have the power to do the same.

In summary, act on purpose, track the process, challenge the lie, prove the truth, celebrate the victories, actively define each outcome and acknowledge what it means about you. You really CAN overcome any challenge set before you. After every success, embrace the positive feelings and complete the following statement: "This action and outcome means that I…"

***"This action and outcome means that I…"***

**Act Method #3: Put Up Safeguards**

Change requires consistency. We need to break down and replace our old habitual ways of thinking, believing and acting. But every time we go off-track, we reinforce the old stories and make change just a little bit more difficult.

I don't expect you to be perfect, because we all make mistakes. However, it's critical that you protect yourself from preventable setbacks. Your new stories offer tremendous potential for your life, but they are vulnerable to attack. You need to set up a perimeter that keeps out the pests that want to dig up your new roots before they take hold.

Plan for resistance to change and protect your new stories with black and white safeguards. In the previous method you turned your stories into actions to do. Now it's time to turn them into actions to *never do*. As you now know, you identify with whatever you do most, so steer yourself in the right direction and away from the things that will pull you off-track.

***Turn your new stories into actions you will never do.***

Whenever we begin to experience success in a difficult area, we often start to feel invincible. We allow the positive feelings to cloud our judgment as we walk right to the edge of destruction, thinking we will be fine. Perhaps you go to the bar for just one drink, into the bakery for a healthy menu item or out for dinner with an old flame. All of these things may seem fine on the surface, but why put yourself in situations that encourage failure or, at the very least, a setback? It's great to practice your resolve with little tests, but some things are just too much too soon.

Successful people create personal standards that they refuse to violate. They establish boundaries to keep themselves safe. As we already discussed, our beliefs change by tiny increments. Just because you believe something today doesn't mean you will have the same conviction a year from now. It is often the little choices and compromises that ruin us, not the big ones. So if you're serious about personal victory, you need safeguards that determine what you will *never do* and where you will *never go* in order to keep yourself on track.

***Successful people create personal standards that they refuse to violate.***

If you were truly courageous, strong, kind, loving or active, what would you never do? Where would you never go? What if you truly valued family, health, compassion and respect? What lines would you draw in the sand?

Here are a few safeguard examples.

Identity Safeguards:

| I am… | Rules |
|---|---|
| Healthy | Never go to a holiday function without having a healthy snack first.<br>Don't fill your cupboards with junk food. |
| Disciplined | Block out non-negotiable personal time in your daily schedule for personal development. (Except for family emergencies.)<br>Never put yourself in impossibly tempting situations like going to a bar if you have a history of drinking. |

Value Safeguards:

| I value… | Rules |
|---|---|
| Marriage | Never spend time alone with someone of the opposite sex, other than family, after 7pm unless your spouse is comfortable with it.<br>Don't work late more than 3 nights per week.<br>Set up family-safe filters on your web browser. |
| Financial Stability | Set a weekly budget and don't go over for any reason other than a family emergency.<br>Don't go to the mall with a credit card in your pocket. |

Worldview Safeguards:

| I believe… | Rules |
|---|---|
| Beauty is in the eye of the beholder | Don't read trashy magazines.<br>Limit your time with people who obsess over their appearance. |
| Life is cause and effect | Set a daily limit on time spent doing non-productive activities like watching television or reading magazines. |

Pathway Safeguards:

| **I commit…** | **Rules** |
|---|---|
| To always give my best effort. | Don't stay up past 10pm on weeknights, so you can always feel rested.<br>Determine how many projects you can handle at once, and say no to everything else. |
| If I take regular breaks, then I will get more done. | Avoid working for more than 3 hours without going for a walk to clear your head.<br>Never work through your lunch break. |

What you will never do is just as important as what you must do, so don't be too proud to set restrictions on yourself. You'll be glad you did.

# EPILOGUE
# NOW WHAT?

Congratulations! You made it to the end. I genuinely hope and trust that Free to Change has made a difference in your life. My goal in writing it was not to make you feel good or to simply fill your head with new information. Instead, my purpose was to help inspire change in your life and to provide the tools to do so.

In the end, action is really all that matters. Now that you have greater insight into your own heart and mind, along with the things that have been holding you back, you can take positive steps towards big change.

At this point in your journey, it's still not about the outcome. Rather, it's about the process and what you will learn to believe. The act of achieving a single goal is a temporary victory, but changing your heart stories is what creates lasting transformation.

What does this mean? From now on, give everything you do and every experience you have a meaning that empowers you. Use everyday life as evidence of who you really are, what you really value, how the world really works and to what you are truly committed. You have the power and responsibility, and with God's help you *will* become unstoppable at whatever you put your mind towards.

## Grow Step-by-Step, Rung-by-Rung

Even though the promise of success is real, tough times will come your way. In the wise words of Dan Carter, a man whom I deeply respect, "life is hard because it's so valuable." Personal transformation is a process. Sometimes it happens in a moment and sometimes it takes a lot of hard work. But in every occasion, it's worth it because life is valuable, and so are you.

You are a multitude of beliefs that are always shifting and changing, climbing up the ladder of personal growth. Your highest and truest self is awaiting you at the top. Your transformation happens in increments of one truth, one experience and one breakthrough at a time.

Every new day is offering you another opportunity to go up. As you see the vision of who you are meant to be, you can live as though you already are. Start by being the person who eats breakfast every day. Then become the person who exercises once, twice and then three times a week. Expand your self-concept, deepen your values, widen your worldview and redirect your pathways by choice, each and every day. It's the little things, and the stories you tell about them, that move the mountain of your life.

***It's the little things, and the stories you tell about them, that move the mountain of your life.***

Use the tools you need to create the heart change you want and start climbing. It isn't necessary to use them all, so don't be overwhelmed. Follow the four major steps, apply the ones you know will make a difference in your life, build your plan and start to live on purpose.

Welcome to the first page of your new life story.

# REFERENCES


## Chapter 1

1. Hudson, Arthur. Consciousness: physiological dependence on rapid memory access. Frontiers in Bioscience 14, 2779-2800, January 1, 2009
2. Confirmation bias: A ubiquitous phenomenon in many guises. Review of General Psychology 2(2), 175–220. Owad, T. (2006, January 4)
3. Source: http://www.npr.org/templates/story/story.php?storyId=104310443

## Chapter 3

1. Free to be you and me: a climate of authenticity alleviates burnout from emotional labor. http://www.ncbi.nlm.nih.gov/pubmed/21875210
2. Baumeister, R. F. (2003). Ego depletion and self-regulation failure: a resource model of self-control. Alcohol Clin Exp Res. 27(2):281-4.
3. Self-affirmation and self-control: affirming core values counteracts ego depletion. http://www.ncbi.nlm.nih.gov/pubmed/19309201

## Chapter 11

1. Ersner-Hershfield, Hal et al. Saving for the future: Neural measures of future self-continuity predict temporal discounting. http://scan.oxfordjournals.org/content/4/1/85.abstract
2. Wilson, Anne E et al. Basking in projected glory: The role of subjective temporal distance in future self-appraisal. http://onlinelibrary.wiley.com/doi/10.1002/ejsp.1863/abstract

## Chapter 13

1. Schoenewolf, G., (1990). Emotional contagion: Behavioral induction in individuals and groups.' 'Modern Psychoanalysis; 15, 49-61
2. Rosenthal, Robert; Jacobson, Lenore. (2003). Pygmalion in the Classroom: Teacher Expectation and Pupils' Intellectual Development.
3. Eden, Dov. (1992). "Leadership and expectations: Pygmalion effects and other self-fulfilling prophecies in organizations," The Leadership Quarterly. 3(4): 271-305 (Winter 1992).
4. N.A. Christakis and J.H. Fowler, "The Spread of Obesity in a Large Social Network Over 32 Years," New England Journal of Medicine 357(4): 370-379 (July 2007).
5. Liljenquist, K. Zhong, C-B. Galinsky, A.D. (2010). The smell of virtue: clean scents promote reciprocity and charity. Psychological Science, 21, 381-383.
6. The Multiple Self-aspects Framework: Self-concept representation and its implications. – Dr. Allen R McConnell: http://allenmcconnell.net/pdfs/msf-PSPR-2011.pdf

## Chapter 14

1. Robbins, A. (2008). Creating Lasting Change.
2. Kleinke, C.L., Peterson, T.R., & Rutledge, T.R. (1998). Effects of self-generated facial expressions on mood. Journal of Personality and Social Psychology, 74, 272-279.

# About the Author

Matthew is a speaker, trainer and marketing guy with a love for all things health and high performance. He is fascinated by human behaviour and all the crazy reasons why we sabotage ourselves and stay stuck in lives we don't like.

Matthew's formal training in business and holistic nutrition. He has a love for big ideas, simple solutions and achieving what used to be impossible. Much of what he writes and speaks on are related to the following core beliefs:

**1. Life is built on principles.**

The world can be confusing and unpredictable, but when you understand the natural laws that govern life, you can start to establish some predictability and stop being pushed around by circumstances. These principles are ours to be discovered and put to use for our own good.

**2. Greatness is received at birth and lived by choice.**

Significance isn't earned or given by others; it's something you've always possessed. Your own unique greatness is there to be uncovered and expressed without apology, but it requires your involvement. It's possible to live a life that matters to you, contributes to the lives of those you love and makes a real impact in the world around you.

### 3. Change doesn't have to feel so hard.

The more you learn to be a leader in your own life, the less you feel bullied by the invisible forces that try to control you. Sometimes it requires inner work, while other times you can use simple life hacks that produce quick, painless results.

### Stay in Touch

If you want to stay connected with Matthew, you can find him online at www.MatthewTaylor.online.

# NOTES

# Notes

# NOTES

# Notes